Satan
A Defeated Foe

Satan

A Defeated Foe

Charles H. Spurgeon

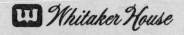 Whitaker House

SATAN A DEFEATED FOE

ISBN: 0-88368-267-2
Printed in the United States of America
Copyright © 1993 by Whitaker House

Whitaker House
30 Hunt Valley Circle
New Kensington, PA 15068

4 5 6 7 8 9 10 11 12 13 14 15 / 06 05 04 03 02 01 00 99 98 97

Contents

Satan Considering
the Saints

Then the Lord said to Satan, "Have you considered My servant Job."
—Job 1:8

How very uncertain are all terrestrial things! How foolish would that believer be who should lay up his treasure anywhere except in heaven! Job's prosperity promised as much stability as anything can beneath the moon. Doubtless, the man had round about him a large household of devoted and attached servants. He had accumulated wealth of a kind which does not suddenly depreciate in value. He had oxen, asses, and cattle. He did not have go to markets or fairs and trade with his goods to procure food and clothing. He carried on the processes of agriculture on a very large scale around his own homestead, and probably grew within his own territory everything that his establishment required. His children were numerous enough to promise a long line of descendants. His prosperity wanted nothing for its consolidation. It had come to its flood-tide: where was the cause which could make it ebb?

Up there, beyond the clouds, where no human eye could see, there was a scene enacted which heralded no good for Job's prosperity. The spirit of evil stood face to face with the infinite Spirit of all good. An extraordinary conversation took place between these two beings.

When called to account for his doings, the evil one boasted that he had gone *"to and fro on the earth, and...[walked] back and forth on it"* (Job 1:7), insinuating that he had met with no hindrance to his will, and found no one to oppose his freely moving and acting at his own pleasure. He had marched everywhere like a king in his own dominions, unhindered and unchallenged.

The great God reminded him that there was at least one place among men where he had no foothold and where his power was unrecognized, namely, in the heart of Job. There was one man who stood like an impregnable castle, garrisoned by integrity, and held with perfect loyalty as the possession of the King of Heaven. The evil one defied Jehovah to try the faithfulness of Job by telling Him that the patriarch's integrity was due to his prosperity, and that he served God and shunned evil from sinister motives because he found his conduct profitable to himself. The God of heaven took up the challenge of the evil one, and gave him permission to take away all the mercies which he affirmed to be the props of Job's integrity. God allowed him to pull down all the outworkings and buttresses and see whether the tower would not stand in its own inherent strength without them. In consequence of this, all Job's wealth went in one black day and not even a child was left to whisper comfort.

A second interview between the Lord and his fallen angel took place. Job was again the subject of conversation. The Great One, again defied by Satan, permitted him even to touch Job in his bone and in his flesh, till the prince became worse than a pauper. He who was rich and happy was poor and wretched, filled with disease from head to foot, and reduced to scraping himself with a miserable potsherd to gain a poor relief from his pain.

Let us see in this the mutability of all earthly things. *"He has founded it upon the seas"* (Psalm 24:2) is David's description of this world. If it is founded on the seas, can you wonder that it changes often? Put not your trust in anything beneath the stars. Remember that "change" is written on the forefront of nature. Do not say therefore, "My mountain stands firm: it shall never be moved." The glance of Jehovah's eye can shake your mountain into dust, the touch of His foot can make it melt like wax and be altogether up in smoke.

"Set your affection on things above, ...where Christ is sitting at the right hand of God" (Colossians 3:2, 1). Let your heart and your treasure be *"where neither moth nor rust destroys and where thieves do not break in and steal"* (Matthew 6:20).

The words of Bernard may help instruct us: "That is the true and chief joy which is not conceived from the creature, but received from the Creator, which (being once possessed thereof) none can take from thee: compared with which all other pleasure is torment, all joy is grief, sweet things are bitter, all glory is baseness, and all delectable things are despicable."

This is not, however, our subject this morning. Accept thus much as merely an introduction to our main discourse. The Lord said to Satan, *"Have you considered my servant Job?"* Let us deliberate, first, in what sense the evil spirit may be said to consider the people of God. Secondly, let us notice what it is that he considers about them. Thirdly, let us comfort ourselves by the reflection that one who is far above Satan considers us in a higher sense.

Satan's Considerations

First, then, in what sense may Satan be said to consider the people of God?

Certainly not in the usual Biblical meaning of the term *"consider."* *"O Lord, consider my trouble"* (Psalm 9:13). *"Consider my meditation"* (Psalm 5:1). *"Blessed is he who considers the poor"* (Psalm 41:1). Such consideration implies goodwill and a careful inspection of the object of benevolence with regard to a wise distribution of favor. In that sense Satan never considers any. If he has any benevolence, it must be towards himself.

All his considerations of other creatures are of the most malevolent kind. No meteoric flash of good flits across the black midnight of his soul, nor does he consider us as we are told to consider the works of God, that is, in order to derive instruction as to God's wisdom and love and kindness. He does not honor God by what he sees in his works or in his people. It is not with him to *go to the ant, you sluggard! Consider her ways and be wise*" (Proverbs 6:6). Rather he goes to the Christian and considers his ways and becomes more foolishly God's enemy than he was before.

The consideration which Satan pays to God's saints is this: he regards them with wonder when he considers the difference between them and himself. A traitor, when he knows the thorough villainy and the blackness of his own heart, cannot help being astounded when he is forced to believe another man to be faithful. The first resort of a treacherous heart is to believe that all men would be just as treacherous, and are really so at bottom. The traitor thinks that all men are traitors like himself, or would be, if it paid them better than fidelity.

When Satan looks at the Christian and finds him faithful to God and to his truth, he considers him as we should consider a phenomenon—perhaps despising him for his folly, but yet marveling at him and wondering how he can act thus. He seems to say, "I, a prince, a peer of God's parliament, would not submit my will to Jehovah. I thought it better to reign in hell than serve in heaven. I kept not my first estate, but fell from my throne. How is it that these stand? What grace is it which keeps these? I was a vessel of gold, and yet I was broken. These are earthen vessels, but I cannot break them! I could not stand in my glory—what can be the matchless grace which upholds them in their poverty, in their obscurity, in their persecution, still faithful to the God who does not bless and exalt them as He did me!"

It may be that he also wonders at their happiness. He feels within himself a seething sea of misery. There is an unfathomable gulf of anguish within his soul. When he looks at believers, he sees them quiet in their souls, full of peace and happiness, often without any outward means by which they should be comforted, yet rejoicing and full of glory. He goes up and down through the world and possesses great power. There be many slaves to serve him, yet he does not have the happiness of spirit possessed by yonder humble cottager, obscure, unknown, having no servants to wait upon her, but stretched out upon the bed of weakness. He admires and hates the peace which reigns in the believer's soul.

His consideration may go farther than this. Do you not think that he considers them to detect, if possible, any flaw and fault in them, by way of solace to himself? "They are not pure," says he, "these blood bought ones, these elect from before the foundations of the world. They still sin! These adopted children of God, for whom the glorious Son bowed his head and gave up the ghost! Even they offend!"

How must he chuckle, with such delight as he is capable of, over the secret sins of God's people. If he can see anything in them inconsistent with their profession, anything which appears to be deceitful and thus like himself, he rejoices. Each sin born in the believer's heart cries to him, "My father! My father!" Then he feels something like the joy of fatherhood as he sees his foul offspring. He looks at the *"old man"* in the Christian, and admires the tenacity with which it maintains its hold, the force and vehemence with which it struggles for mastery. He gleefully observes the craft and cunning with which every now and then, at set intervals, at convenient opportunities, the old nature puts forth all its force. He considers our sinful flesh and makes it one of the books in which he diligently reads. One of the fairest prospects the devil's eye ever rests upon is the inconsistency and the impurity which he can discover in the true child of God. In this respect he had very little to consider in God's true servant, Job.

This is just the starting point of his consideration. I do not doubt that he views the Lord's people, and especially the more prominent leaders among them, as the great barriers to the progress of his kingdom. Just as the engineer, endeavoring to make a railway, keeps his eye very much fixed upon the hills and rivers, and especially upon the great mountain through which it will take years laboriously to bore a tunnel, so Satan, in looking upon his various plans to carry on his dominion in the world, considers most such men as Job.

Satan must have thought much about Martin Luther. "I could ride the world over," says he, "if it were not for that monk. He stands in my way. That strong-headed man hates and mauls my firstborn son, the pope. If I could get rid of him I would not mind though fifty thousand smaller saints stood in my way." He is sure to consider God's servant, if there be *"none like him"* (Job 1:8), if he stands out distinct and separate from his fellows. Those of us who are called to the work of the ministry must expect from our position to be the special objects of his consideration. When the magnifying glass is at the eye of that dreadful warrior, he is sure to look out for those who by their uniforms are discovered to be the officers, and he bids his sharp-shooters to be very careful to aim at these. "For," says he, "if the standard-bearer falls, then the victory will be more readily gained for our side, and our opponents shall be readily put to rout."

If you are more generous than other saints, if you live nearer to God than others, as the birds peck most at the ripest fruit, so may you expect Satan to be most busy against you. Who cares to contend for a province covered with stones and barren rocks, and ice-bound by frozen seas? But in all times there is sure to be a contention after the fat valleys where the wheat-sheaves are plenteous, and where the husbandman's toil is well rewarded. Thus, for you who honor God most, Satan will struggle very sternly. He wants to pluck God's jewels from His crown, if he can, and take the Redeemer's precious stones even from the breastplate itself.

Just so he considers God's people. Viewing them as hindrances to his reign, he contrives methods by which he may remove them out of his way or turn them to his own account. Darkness would cover the earth if he could blow out the lights. There would be no fruit to shake like Lebanon if he could destroy that handful of corn upon the top of the mountains. Hence, his perpetual consideration is to make the faithful fall from among men.

It needs not much wisdom to discern that the great object of Satan in considering God's people is to do them injury. I scarcely think he hopes to destroy the really chosen and blood-bought heirs of life. My notion is that he is too good a divine for that. He has been foiled so often when he has attacked God's people, that he can hardly think he shall be able to destroy the elect. You remember the soothsayers who are very nearly related to him spoke to Haman thus, *"If Mordecai, before whom you have begun to fall, is of Jewish descent, you will not prevail against him but will surely fall before him"* (Esther 6:13). He knows very well that there is a royal seed in the land against whom he fights in vain.

It strikes me if he could be absolutely certain that any one soul was chosen of God, he would scarcely waste his time in attempting to destroy it, although he might seek to worry and to dishonor it. However, most likely Satan no more knows who God's elect are than we do, for he can only judge as we do by outward actions, though he can form a more accurate judgment than we can, through longer experience and being able to see persons in private where we cannot intrude. Yet into God's book of secret decrees his black eye can never peer. By their fruits he knows them, and we know them in the same manner.

Since, however, we are often mistaken in our judgment, he too may be also. And it seems to me that he therefore makes it his policy to endeavor to destroy them all—not knowing in which case he may succeed. He goes about *"seeking whom he may devour"* (1 Peter 5:8), and, as he knows not whom he may be permitted to swallow up, he attacks all the people of God with vehemence.

Someone may say, "How can one devil do this?" He does not do it by himself alone. I do not know that many of us have ever been tempted directly by Satan: we may not be notable enough among men to be worth his trouble, but he has a whole host of inferior spirits under his supremacy and control. As the centurion said of himself, so he might have said of Satan, *"[He says to this spirit], 'Go,' and he goes; and to another, 'Come,' and he comes; and to my servant, 'Do this,' and he does it"* (Matthew 8:9). Thus all the servants of God will more or less come under the direct or indirect assaults of the great enemy of souls, and that with a view of destroying them. For he would, if it were possible, deceive the very elect.

Where he cannot destroy, there is no doubt that Satan's object is to worry. He does not like to see God's people happy. I believe the devil greatly delights in some ministers, whose tendency in their preaching is to multiply and foster doubts and fears, and grief and despondency as the evidences of God's people. "Ah," says the devil, "preach on. You are doing my work well, for I like to see God's people mournful. If I can make them hang their harps on the willows and go about with miserable faces, I reckon I have done my work very completely."

My dear friends, let us watch against those specious temptations which pretend to make us humble, but which really aim at making us unbelieving. Our God takes no delight in our suspicions and mistrusting. See how He proves His love in the gift of his dear Son Jesus. Banish then all your ill-surmising, and rejoice in unmoved confidence. God delights to be worshiped with joy. *"Oh come, let us sing to the Lord! Let us shout joyfully to the Rock of our salvation. Let us come before His presence with thanksgiving; Let us shout joyfully to Him with psalms"* (Psalm 95:1-2). *"Be glad in the LORD and rejoice, you righteous; and shout for joy, all you upright in heart"* (Psalm 32:11). *"Rejoice in the Lord always. Again I will say, rejoice"* (Philippians 4:4). Satan does not like this.

Martin Luther used to say, "Let us sing psalms and spite the devil." I have no doubt Martin Luther was pretty nearly right, for that lover of discord hates harmonious, joyous praise. Beloved brother, the arch-enemy wants to make you wretched here, if he cannot have you hereafter. In this, no doubt, he is aiming a blow at the honor of God. He is well aware that mournful Christians often dishonor the faithfulness of God by mistrusting it. Thus he thinks if he can worry us until we no more believe in the constancy and goodness of the Lord, he shall have robbed God of His praise. *"Whoever offers praise, glorifies Me,"* (Psalm 50:23), says God. So Satan lays the axe at the root of our praise, that God may cease to be glorified.

Moreover, if Satan cannot destroy a Christian, how often has he spoiled his usefulness? Many a believer has fallen, not to break his neck—that is impossible—but he has broken some important bone and has gone limping to his grave! We can recall with grief some men who were once prominent in the church and who were running well, but who suddenly through the stress of temptation fell into sin. Their names were never mentioned in the church again except with bated breath. Everybody thought and prayed that they were saved as by the fire, but certainly their former usefulness never could return. It is very easy to go back in the heavenly pilgrimage, but it is very hard to retrieve your steps.

You may soon turn aside and put out your candle, but you cannot light it quite so speedily. Friend, beloved in the Lord, watch against the attacks of Satan and stand fast, because you, as a pillar in the house of God, are very dear to us. We cannot spare you. As a father or as a matron in our midst, we honor you, and we do not wish to mourn and lament or to be grieved by hearing the shouts of our adversaries while they cry, "Aha! Aha! So would we have it!" Alas! There have been many things done in our Zion which we should *tell it not in Gath, proclaim it not in the streets of Askelon, lest the daughters of the Philistines rejoice, lest the daughters of the uncircumcised triumph"* (2 Samuel 1:20).

May God grant us grace as a church to stand against the wiles of Satan and his attacks, that having done his worst, he may gain no advantage over us. After having considered, reconsidered, and counted well our towers and bulwarks, may he be compelled to retire because his battering rams cannot jar so much as a stone from our ramparts, and his slings cannot slay one single soldier on the walls.

Before I leave this point, I should like to say that perhaps it may be suggested, "How is it that God permits this constant and malevolent consideration of His people by the evil one?" One answer doubtless is that God knows what is for His own glory, and that He gives no account of His matters. Having permitted free agency, and having allowed for some mysterious reason the existence of evil, it does not seem agreeable with His having done so to destroy Satan, but He gives him power that it may be a fair hand-to-hand fight between sin and holiness, between grace and craftiness.

Also, let it be remembered that, incidentally, the temptations of Satan are of service to the people of God. Fenelon says that they are the file which rubs off much of the rust of self-confidence. I may add, they are the horrible sound in the sentinel's ear, which is sure to keep him awake. An experimental theologian remarks that there is no temptation in the world which is so bad as not being tempted at all, for to be tempted will tend to keep us awake. Whereas, being without temptation, flesh and blood are weak. Though the spirit may be willing, yet we may be found falling into slumber. Children do not run away from their father's side when big dogs bark at them. The howlings of the devil may tend to drive us nearer to Christ, may teach us our own weakness, may keep us upon our own watch tower, and be made the means of preservation from other ills. Let us *"be sober, be vigilant; because your adversary the devil walks about like a roaring lion, seeking whom he may devour"* (1 Peter 5:8).

May we who are in a prominent position be permitted affectionately to press upon you one earnest request. *"Brethren, pray for us"* (1 Thessalonians 5:25), that exposed as we are peculiarly to the consideration of Satan, we may be guarded by divine power. Let us be made rich by your faithful prayers that we may be kept even to the end.

Satan's Injurious View

Secondly, specifically what does Satan consider with a view towards the injury of God's people?

It cannot be said of him, as it is of God, that he knows us totally. However, since he has been now nearly six thousand years dealing with poor fallen humanity, he must have acquired a very vast experience in that time. Having been all over the earth, and having tempted the highest and the lowest, he must know exceedingly well what the springs of human action are and how to play upon them.

Satan watches and considers first of all our peculiar infirmities. He looks us up and down, just as I have seen a horse dealer do with a horse. He soon finds out where we are faulty. I, a common observer, might think the horse an exceedingly good one as I see it running up and down the road, but the dealer sees what I cannot see and knows how to handle the creature in such quarters and at such points that he soon discovers any hidden mischief. Satan knows how to look at us and size us up from heel to head, so that he says of this man, "His infirmity is lust," of that one, "He has a quick temper," of another, "He is proud," or of that other, "He is slothful." The eye of malice is very quick to perceive a weakness, and the hand of enmity soon takes advantage of it. When the arch-spy finds a weak place in the walls of our castles, he takes care where to plant his battering ram and begin his siege. You may conceal, even from your dearest friend, your infirmity, but you will not conceal it from your worst enemy. He has lynx eyes and detects in a moment the weak point in your armor. He goes about with a match, and though you may think you have covered all the gunpowder of your heart, yet he knows how to find a crack to put his match through. Much mischief will he do, unless eternal mercy prevents.

He takes care also to consider our frames and states of mind. If the devil would attack us when our minds are in certain moods, we would be more than a match for him. He knows this and shuns the encounter. Some men are more vulnerable to temptation when they are distressed and desponding. The fiend will then assail them. Others will be more liable to catch fire when they are jubilant and full of joy, so that is when he will strike his spark into the tinder. Certain persons, when they are overly vexed and tossed to and fro, can be made to say almost anything. Others, when their souls are like perfectly placid waters, are just then in a condition to be navigated by the devil's vessel.

As the worker in metals knows that one metal is to be worked at a particular heat and another at a different temperature, as those who have to deal with chemicals know that at a certain heat one fluid will boil while another reaches the boiling-point much earlier, so Satan knows exactly the temperature at which to work us to his purpose. Small pots boil quickly when they are put on the fire, and so are little men of quick temper soon in a passion. Larger vessels require more time and coal before they will boil, but when they do, it is a boil indeed, not soon forgotten or abated.

The enemy, like a fisherman, watches his fish, adapts his bait to his prey, and knows in what seasons and times the fish are most likely to bite. This hunter of souls comes unawares. Often we are overtaken in a fault or caught in a trap through an unwatchful frame of mind. That rare collector of choice sayings, Thomas Spencer, has the following, which is much to the point:

"The chameleon, when he lies on the grass to catch flies and grasshoppers, taketh upon him the color of the grass, as the polypus doth the color of the rock under which he lurks, that the fish may boldly come near him without any suspicion of danger. In like manner, Satan turns himself into that shape which we least fear, and sets before us such objects of temptation as are most agreeable to our natures, that so he may the sooner draw us into his net; he sails with every wind, and blows us that way which we incline ourselves through the weakness of nature. Is our knowledge in matter of faith deficient? He tempts us to error. Is our conscience tender? He tempts us to scrupulosity, and too much preciseness. Hath our conscience, like the ecliptic line, some latitude? He tempts us to carnal liberty. Are we bold spirited? He tempts us to presumption. Are we timorous and distrustful? He tempts us to desperation. Are we of a flexible disposition? He tempts us to inconstancy. Are we stiff? He labors to make obstinate heretics, schismatics, or rebels of us. Are we of an austere temper? He tempts us to cruelty. Are we soft and mild? He tempts us to indulgence and foolish pity. Are we hot in matters of religion? Ire tempts us to blind zeal and superstition. Are we cold? He tempts us to Laodicean lukewarmness. Thus doth he lay his traps, that one way or other, he may ensnare us."

He also takes care to consider our position among men. There are a few persons who are most easily tempted when they are alone. They are then subjected to great heaviness of mind, and they may be driven to most awful crimes. Perhaps most of us are more liable to sin when we are in company. In some company I never would be led into sin; into another society I could scarcely venture. Many are so full of levity that those of us who are inclined the same way can scarcely look them in the face without feeling our own besetting sin rising. Others are so somber that if they meet a brother of like mind, they are pretty sure between them to invent an evil report of the good land. Satan knows where to overtake you in a place where you lie open to his attacks. He will pounce upon you, swooping like a bird of prey from the sky, where he has been watching for the time to make his descent with prospect of success.

How, too, he considers our condition in the world! He looks at one man and says, "That man has property: it is of no use my trying these certain deceits with him. But here is another man who is very poor, I will catch him in that net." Then, again, he looks at the poor man and says, "Now, I cannot tempt him to this folly, but I will lead the rich man into it." As the sportsman has one gun for wild fowl and another for deer and game, so has Satan a different temptation for various orders of men. I do not suppose that the Queen's temptation ever will annoy the kitchen-maid. I do not suppose, on the other hand, that the maid's temptation will ever be very serious to me. Probably you could escape from mine, though I do not think you could. I sometimes fancy I could bear yours, though I question if I could. Satan knows, however, just where to smite each of us. Our position, our capabilities, our education, our standing in society, our calling—all may be doors through which he may attack us.

You who nave no calling at all are in peculiar peril. I wonder the devil does not swallow you outright. The most likely man to go to hell is the man who has nothing to do on earth. I say that seriously. I believe that there cannot happen a much worse evil to a person than to be placed where he has no work. If I should ever be in such a state, I would get employment at once for fear I should be carried off, body and soul, by the evil one. Idle people tempt the devil to tempt them.

Let us have something to do; let us keep our minds occupied. If not, we make room for the devil. Industry will not make us gracious, but the lack of work may make us vicious. Have always something on the anvil or in the file.

> "In books, or work, or healthful play,
>   I would be busy too,
> For Satan finds some mischief still
>   For idle hands to do."

So Watts taught us in our childhood, and so let us believe in our adulthood. Books, work, or such recreations as are necessary for health should occupy our time. For if I throw myself down in indolence, like an old piece of iron, I must not wonder that I grow rusty with sin.

Nor have I finished yet. Satan, when he makes his investigations, notices all the objects of our affection. I do not doubt that when he went around Job's house, he observed it as carefully as thieves do a jeweller's premises when they are planning to break into them. They very cunningly take account of every door, window, and lock. They do not fail to look at the house next door, for they may have to reach the treasure through the building which adjoins it.

When the devil looked around, jotting down in his mind all Job's position, he thought to himself, "There are the camels and the oxen, the asses, and the servants —yes, I can use all these very admirably." "Then," he thought, "there are the three daughters! There are the seven sons, and they all go feasting. I know where to catch them, and if I can just blow the house down when they are partying, that will afflict the father's mind more severely, for he will say 'O that they had died when they had been praying, rather than when they had been feasting and drinking wine.'"

"I will put down too in the inventory," says the devil, "his wife. I dare say I shall want her," and accordingly it came to that. Nobody could have done what Job's wife did. None of the servants could have said that sad sentence so stingingly, or—if she meant it very kindly—none could have said it with such a fascinating air as Job's own wife. *"Bless God and die,"* as it may be read, or more usually, *"Curse God and die"* (Job 2:9). Oh, Satan, you have plowed with Job's heifer, but you have not succeeded; Job's strength lies in his God, not in his hair, or else you might have shaved him as Samson was shorn!

Perhaps the evil one had even inspected Job's personal sensitivities, and so selected that form of bodily affliction which he knew to be most dreaded by his victim. He brought upon him a disease which Job may have seen and shuddered at, in poor men outside the city gates.

Brethren, Satan knows quite as much in regard to you. You have a child, and Satan knows that you idolize it. "Ah," says he, "there is a place for my wounding him." Even the partner of your bosom may be made a quiver in which hell's arrows shall be stored till the time may come, and then she may prove the bow from which Satan will shoot them. Watch even your neighbor and she that lies in your bosom, for you know not how Satan may get an advantage over you.

Our habits, our joys, our sorrows, our retirements, our public positions—all may be made weapons of attack by this desperate foe of the Lord's people. We have snares everywhere, in our beds and at our tables, in our houses and in the street. There are snares and traps in company; there are pits when we are alone. We may find temptations in the house of God as well as in the world, traps in our high estate, and deadly poisons in our abasement. We must not expect to be rid of temptations till we have crossed the Jordan, and then, thank God, we are beyond gunshot of the enemy. The last howling of the dog of hell will be heard as we descend into the chilly waters of the black stream, but when we hear the hallelujah of the glorified, we shall have finished with the black prince forever and ever.

Higher Considerations

Satan considered, but there was a higher consideration which overrode his consideration.

In times of war, the military strategists and mine specialists of one side will lay out a mine field. It is a very common counteraction for the the other side to countermine by undermining the first mines. This is just what God does with Satan. Satan is laying mines, and he thinks to light the fuse and blow up God's building. But all the while God is undermining him, and he blows up his own mine before he can do any real mischief.

The devil is the greatest of all fools. He has more knowledge but less wisdom than any other creature. He is more subtle than all the beasts of the field, but it is well called subtlety, not wisdom. It is not true wisdom; it is only another shape of folly.

All the while that Satan was tempting Job, he little knew that he was answering God's purpose, for God was looking on and considering the whole of it and holding the enemy as a man holds a horse by its bridle. The Lord had considered exactly how far he would let Satan go.

The first time, He did not permit him to touch Job's flesh—perhaps that was more than Job at that time could have borne. Have you ever noticed that if you are in good strong bodily health you can bear losses and crosses, and even bereavements with something like equanimity? Now that was the case with Job. Perhaps if the disease had come first and the rest had followed, it might have been a temptation too heavy for Job. But God, who knows just how far to let the enemy go, will say to Satan, "Thus far, and no farther."

By degrees Job became accustomed to his poverty; in fact, the trial had lost all its sting the moment he said, *"The Lord gave, and the Lord has taken away."* That enemy was slain. It was buried, and this was the funeral oration, *"Blessed be the name of the Lord"* (Job 1:21).

When the second trial came, the first trial had qualified Job to bear the second. It may be a more severe trial for a man in the possession of great worldly wealth suddenly to be deprived of the bodily power of enjoying it, than to lose all first and then lose the health necessary to its enjoyment.

Having already lost all, Job might almost have said, "I thank God that now I have nothing to enjoy, and therefore the loss of the power to enjoy it is not so wearisome. I do not have to say, 'How I wish I could go out in my fields and see to my servants,' for they are all dead. I do not wish to see my children; they are all dead and gone. I am thankful that they are. Better so, than that they should see their poor father sit on a dunghill like this."

He might have been almost glad if his wife had gone too, for certainly it was not a particularly merciful blessing when she was spared. Possibly, if he had had all his children about him, it might have been a harder trial than it was. The Lord, who weighs mountains in scales, had meted out his servant's woe.

Did not the Lord also consider how He would sustain his servant under the trial? Beloved, you do not know how blessedly our God poured the secret oil upon Job's fire of grace while the devil was throwing buckets of water on it. He said to Himself, "If Satan shall do much, I will do more. If he takes away much, I will give more. If he tempts the man to curse, I will fill him so full of love for Me that He shall bless me. I will help him; I will strengthen him; yes, I will uphold him with the right hand of my righteousness." (See Isaiah 41:10.)

Christian, take those two thoughts and put them under your tongue as a wafer made with honey. You will never be tempted without express license from the throne where Jesus pleads. On the other hand, when He permits it, He will with the temptation make a way of escape or give you grace to stand under it.

In the next place, the Lord considered how to sanctify Job by this trial. Job was a much better man at the end of the story than he was at the beginning. *"That man was blameless and upright"* (Job 1:1) at first, but there was a little pride about him. We are poor creatures to criticize such a man as Job, but still there was in him a sprinkling of self-righteousness, I think, which his friends brought out. Eliphaz and Zophar said such irritating things that poor Job could not help replying in strong terms about himself that were rather too strong. There was a little too much self-justification in his self-defense.

He was not proud, as some of us are, of a very little. He had much to be proud of, at least in the eyes of the world, but yet there was the tendency to be exalted with it. Though the devil did not know it, perhaps if he had left Job alone, that pride might have run to seed, and Job might have sinned. However, he was in such a hurry that he would not let the bad seed ripen, but hastened to cut it up. So it became the Lord's tool to bring Job into a more humble, and consequently, a more safe and blessed state of mind.

Moreover, observe how Satan was a lackey to the Almighty! Job all this while was being enabled to earn a greater reward. All his prosperity was not enough. God loved Job so much, that He intended to give him twice the property. He intended to give him his children again. He meant to make him more famous man than ever, a man whose name would ring down through the ages, a man who will be talked of through all generations. He was not to be the man of Uz, but of the whole world. He was not to be heard of by a handful in one neighborhood, but all men are to hear of Job's patience in the hour of trial.

Who was to do this? Who was to fashion the trumpet of fame through which Job's name would be blown? The devil went to the forge and worked away with all his might to make Job illustrious! Foolish devil! He was piling up a pedestal on which God would set his servant Job, that he may be looked upon with wonder by all ages.

To conclude, Job's afflictions and Job's patience have been a lasting blessing to the church of God, and they have inflicted incredible disgrace upon Satan. If you want to make the devil angry, throw the story of Job in his face. If you desire to have your own confidence sustained, may God the Holy Ghost lead you into the patience of Job. How many saints have been comforted in their distress by this story of patience! How many have been saved out of the jaw of the lion and from the paw of the bear by the dark experiences of the patriarch of Uz. O arch-fiend, how you are taken in your own net! You have thrown a stone which has fallen on your own head. You made a pit for Job, but have fallen into it yourself. You are taken in your own craftiness. Jehovah has made fools of the wise and driven the diviners mad.

Brethren, let us commit ourselves in faith to the care and keeping of God. Come poverty, come sickness, come death, we will in all things through Jesus Christ's blood be conquerors. By the power of His Spirit, we shall overcome at the last. I pray that we were all trusting in Jesus. May those who have not trusted Him be led to begin this very morning. And God shall have all the praise in us all, forevermore. Amen.

2

Satan in a Rage

Now a great sign appeared in heaven: a woman clothed with the sun, with the moon under her feet, and on her head a garland of twelve stars. Then being with child, she cried out in labor and in pain to give birth.

And another sign appeared in heaven: behold a great, fiery red dragon having seven heads and ten horns, and seven diadems on his heads. His tail drew a third of the stars of heaven and threw them to the earth. And the dragon stood before the woman who was ready to give birth, to devour her Child as soon as it was born.

And she bore a male Child who was to rule all nations with a rod of iron. And

her Child was caught up to God and to
His throne.
Then the woman fled into the wilderness,
where she has a place prepared by God,
that they should feed her there one
thousand two hundred and sixty days.
And war broke out in heaven: Michael
and his angels fought against the dragon;
and the dragon and his angels fought, but
they did not prevail, nor was a place
found for them in heaven any longer.
So the great dragon was cast out,
that old serpent of old, called the Devil
and Satan, who deceives the whole world;
he was cast to the earth,
and his angels were cast out with him.
Then I heard a loud voice saying in
heaven, "Now salvation, and strength,
and the kingdom of our God, and the
power of His Christ have come, for the
accuser of our brethren, who accused them
before our God day and night, has been
cast down. And they overcame him by the
blood of the Lamb and by the word of
their testimony, and they did not love
their lives to the death.
"Therefore rejoice, O heavens and
you who dwell in them!

*Woe to the inhabitants of the earth and
the sea! For the devil has come down to
you, having great wrath, because he
knows that he has a short time."
Now when the dragon saw that he had
been cast to the earth, he persecuted the
woman who gave birth to the male Child.
But the woman was given two wings of a
great eagle, that she might fly into the
wilderness to her place, where she is
nourished for a time and times and half a
time, from the presence of the serpent.
So the serpent spewed water out of his
mouth like a flood after the woman, that
he might cause her to be carried away by
the flood. But the earth helped the
woman, and the earth opened its mouth
and swallowedup the flood which the
dragon had spewed out of its mouth.
And the dragon was enraged with the
woman, and he went to make war on the
rest of her offspring, who keep the
commandments of God and have the
testimony of Jesus Christ.
—Revelation 12:1-17*

T he great battle in the heavenlies has
been fought. Our glorious Michael has

forever overthrown the dragon and cast him down. In the highest regions the great principle of evil has received a total defeat through the life and death of our Lord Jesus. For human sin atonement has been made, and the great quarrel between God and man has come to a happy end. Everlasting righteousness has been brought in, and the peace of God reigns in heaven. The conflict henceforth rages here below. In these inferior regions the prince of this world is warring mightily against the cause of God and truth. Much woe does this cause to the sons of men, woe which will never end till his power is altogether taken away.

Observe concerning our arch-enemy that he exercises forethought and care as to the evil enterprise to which he has set his hand. Whatever foolish men may do, the devil is thinking. Others may be heedless and thoughtless, but he is anxious and full of consideration. He knows that his time or "opportunity" is short. He looks ahead to its close, for he is no careless waster of time and forgetter of the end. He values his opportunity to maintain his kingdom, to distress the people of God, and to dishonor the name of Christ. Since it is but a short time, he treats it as such.

He infers the brevity of his time from the victory which Jesus has already gained over him. In reading the chapter, we saw how the Child who is to rule all nations with a rod of iron was caught up to God and to his throne. Then we saw the war in heaven and how the devil was cast out into the earth and his angels were cast out with him. Then a loud voice was heard on high, *"Now salvation, and strength, and the kingdom of our God, and the power of His Christ have come, for the accuser of our brethren, who accused them before our God day and night, has been cast down"* (Revelation 12:10). Very well may the old serpent conclude that he will be routed on earth since he has already sustained so dire a defeat that he has fallen from heaven, never to rise again. Because the manchild Christ Jesus has met him in conflict, met him when as yet all his power was unbroken, and has cast him down from his high places, he is persuaded that his reign is ended and that his opportunity is short.

Satan feels about him even now a chain which is lengthened for awhile, but which shall be drawn up shorter about him and tightened down by-and-by. Then he shall roam the earth no longer, but lie as a captive in his prison house. Fallen as this apostate spirit has become, he has wit enough to look forward to the future. Oh, that men were half as wise and would remember their end. I beg you to notice this fact concerning the evil spirit, that you too may learn to acquire knowledge and then use it for practical purposes. Why should it always be that the powers of darkness appear to act more wisely than the children of light? For once I would point out a matter in which our worst foe may teach us a lesson.

Among men there are some who know a great many important matters but act as if they did not know them. Their knowledge is so much waste stored up in the lumber-room of their minds and never brought into the workshop to be used for practical purposes.

For instance, we know our mortality and yet live as if we were never meant to die. There is great necessity for many of us to pray, *"So teach us to number our days, that we may gain a heart of wisdom"* (Psalm 90:12). We must know that our time is short and that our life will soon come to an end, and yet we fail to know it practically, for we are not as earnest as dying men ought to be. In this the arch-enemy is not so foolish as we are, for he so well knows that his time is short that he remembers the fact and is activated by it.

Note well the direction in which this knowledge operates upon him. It excites his emotions. The deepest emotion of which he is capable is that of anger, for he knows not how to love. Wrath is his very soul, as hatred is his very life. He knows nothing of gentleness, nothing of affection, and there-fore the fact that his time is short stirs the master passion within him, and he has great wrath. His evil nature is all on fire, and his excitement is terrible.

How much the shortness of our time ought to still our hearts! With what ar-dency of love and fervency of zeal ought we to pass the days of our sojourning here! Knowing that the time of our departure is at hand, and that the season in which we can serve God among the sons of men is very brief, we ought to be excited to flam-ing zeal and passionate love. We are not half as stirred as we ought to be. Devils feel great hatred. Why is it that we do not feel great love? Shall they be more eager to destroy than we are to save? Shall they be all alive, and shall we be half dead?

Nor is the result of knowing that his time is short merely emotional on the part of the arch-fiend, for in consequence of his great wrath, he is moved to make earnest efforts. His energy is excited, he persecutes the woman whose seed he dreads, and he pours floods out of his mouth against her. There is nothing which Satan can do for his evil cause which he does not do. We may be half-hearted, but he never is. He is the very image of ceaseless industry and indefatigable earnestness. He will do all that can be done in the time of his permitted range. We may be sure that he will never lose a day.

My brethren, you and I, on the other hand, should be moved by the shortness of our opportunity to an equal energy of incessant industry, serving God continually, because *"the night is coming when no one can work"* (John 9:4). My friend, if you want your children brought to Christ, speak to them, for they will soon be without a father. If you wish your servants to be saved, labor for their conversion, for they will soon be without a mistress. If you desire your brother to be converted, speak to him, for your sisterly love will not much longer avail him. Minister, if you would save your congregation by the Spirit of God, seek to do it at once, for your tongue will soon be silent. Teacher in the Sunday-school, if you would have your class gathered into the Good Shepherd's fold, treasure up every Sabbath's opportunities, for in a short time the place which knows you now shall know you no more forever.

Thus, as of old *"the Israelites would go down to the Philistines to sharpen each man's plowshare, his mattock, his ax, and his sickle"* (1 Samuel 13:20), so I have urged you to quicken your diligence by the example of the prince of darkness. Shall we not learn wisdom from his subtlety and zeal from his fury? Shall he discern the signs of the times and therefore bestir himself, while we sleep on? Shall evil encompass the sea and land while the children of God creep about in idleness? God forbid. I beseech you, my brethren, awake out of your sleep and see the great wrath of the old dragon.

The text tells us that the shortness of Satan's opportunity stirs his wrath. We may gather a general rule from this one statement: in proportion as the devil's time is shortened, so his energy is increased. We may take it as an assured fact that when he rages to the uttermost, his opportunities are nearly over. He has great wrath, knowing that his time is short. I hope there will be something of instruction in this, and somewhat of comfort for all those who are on the right side. May the Holy Ghost make it so.

In the world around us we must not consider that things go altogether amiss when the powers of evil become strong. We would be foolish if we wept in despair because the tares are ripening, for is not the wheat ripening too? True, the dead become more corrupt, but if the living become more active, why should we lament? Because blasphemy grows loud, because infidels seek to undermine the foundation of the faith, or because the clouds of superstition grow more dense, we must not therefore conclude that we have fallen upon evil times, the like of which were never seen before.

Oftentimes the development of evil is an indication that there is an equal or a greater development of good, and that the climax of ill is frequently its end. Do you not know that in the world of nature the darkest time of the night is that which precedes the dawning of the day? May it not be the same in the spiritual and moral world? Does not the old proverb tell us concerning the year, that "as the day lengthens, the cold strengthens"? As the spring comes with lengthened days, the frosts often grow more sharp and hard. Is it not also plain to the simplest mind that the turning of the tide happens when the ebb has reached its utmost.

Even so, when evil is at its height, it is nearest to its fall. Look for confirmation to the pages of history. When the quota of bricks was doubled, Moses came to deliver the oppressed. When Pharaoh would by no means let the people go and his yoke seemed riveted upon the neck of Israel, then the right arm of God was made bare, and the Red Sea beheld His vengeance. When despots grow most tyrannical, liberty's hour is coming. When the lie becomes exceeding bold and wears a brazen front, then it is that truth confounds her. When Goliath stalks abroad and defies the armies of Israel, then is the stone already in the sling and the David hard at hand, to lay the giant low. Do not, therefore, dread the advent of greater opposition, nor the apparent increase in strength of those oppositions which already exist, for it has ever been so in the history of events that the hour of the triumph of evil is the hour of its doom. When Belshazzar profanes the holy vessels, the handwriting blazes on the wall. When Haman is at the king's banquet of wine seeking the blood of the whole race of the Jews, the gallows are prepared for him upon his own roof.

It shall be seen, even to the last hour of history, that the devil rages all the more when his empire is nearer to its end. At the very last, he shall go about to deceive the nations which are in the four quarters of the earth, Gog and Magog, to gather them together to battle. They shall come up in great hosts, fierce for the conflict, to *"the battle of that great day of God Almighty"* (Revelation 16:14) at Armageddon. It shall then seem as if the light of Israel must be quenched, and the truth of God utterly extinguished. But in that dread hour, the Lord shall triumph gloriously, and He shall smite his adversaries to their final overthrow. Then shall the angel standing in the sun invite the vultures and all the fowls that fly in the midst of heaven to gather to the grim feast of vengeance, to eat the flesh of horsemen and men of might. Then also shall *"the devil, who deceived them, was cast into the lake of fire and...will be tormented day and night forever and ever"* (Revelation 20:10). Then also shall the shout be heard, *"Alleluia! For the Lord God Omnipotent reigns"* (Revelation 19:6). On the greatest possible scale the greatness of the dragon's wrath is a sure prophecy of the end of his reign.

Now, what is true on a great scale is true on the smaller ones. Missionaries in any country will generally find that the last onslaught of heathenism is the most ferocious. We shall find that whenever falsehood comes into contact with the truth and error is driven to its last entrenchments, they fight for life, tooth and nail, with all their might. The wrath is great because their time is short. In any village or town in England, or in any other country, whenever the opposition to the Gospel reaches its most outrageous pitch and men seem as if they would murder the preacher of the Word, you may reckon that the power of the opposition is almost over.

After the mad fit, active persecution will cease. There will come a time of calm and, perhaps, of general reception of the

Gospel. When once the bad passions of mankind shall have boiled up, they will cool down again. Has not God promised to restrain it? As the burning heat of the noon sun does not last forever, but gradually abates when it has reached the hottest point, so is it with the wrath of man, which the foul fiend so often uses for his base purposes.

The same truth will apply to every individual man. When God begins his great work in a sinner's heart to lead him to Christ, it is no bad sign if the man feels more hatred for God than ever, more dislike for good things than before. Neither need we despair if he is driven into greater sin than ever. The ferocity of the temptation indicates the vigor with which Satan contends for any one of his black sheep. He will not lose his subjects if he can help it, and so he puts forth all his strength to keep them under his power. He is especially diligent and furious when the power of grace is about to prevail for their salvation. I will not, however, dwell upon this point, because it is to be the subject of our discourse.

The general fact is further illustrated in the cases of many believers. There are times when, in the believer's heart, the battle rages horribly. He hardly knows whether he is a child of God at all and is ready to give up all hope. He cannot pray or praise, for he is so distracted. He cannot read the Scriptures without horrible thoughts. It seems as if he must utterly perish, for no space is given him in which to refresh his heart, the attacks are so continual and violent. Such dreadful excitements are often followed by years of peace, quiet usefulness, holiness, and communion with God. Satan knows that God is about to set a limit to his vexations of the good man, and so he rages extremely because his opportunity is short. It is very remarkable that some of the greatest of the saints have died in the midst of the most fearful conflicts from the same reason: the dog howled at them because he knew that they would soon be out of his reach.

You would not suppose that Martin Luther, a man so brave and strong that he could defy the Pope and the devil, should on his dying bed be woefully unsure. Yet it was so: his worst struggle was the closing one. He was more than a conqueror, but the fight was severe, as if the devil, that old coward, waited until he had his antagonist down, waited until he was weak and feeble, and then leaped upon him to worry if he could not devour him. Truly Luther had bothered the devil, and we do not wonder at the malice of the fiend. Satan knew that he would soon be out of the reach of his fiery arrows forever, and therefore he must have a last shot at him.

It was precisely the same case with John Knox. Having been observed to sigh deeply and asked the cause of it, Knox replied:

"I have formerly, during my frail life, sustained many tests and many assaults of Satan, but at present he hath assailed me most fearfully, and put forth all his strength to devour, and make all end of me at once. Often before has he placed my sins before my eyes, often tempted me to despair, often endeavored to ensnare me by the allurements of the world; but these weapons were broken by the sword of the Spirit, the word of God, and the enemy failed. Now he has attacked me in another way: the cunning serpent has labored to persuade me that I have merited heaven and eternal blessedness by the faithful discharge of my ministry. But, blessed be God, who has enabled me to beat down and quench this fiery dart by suggesting to me such passages of Scripture as these: *'What hast thou that thou hast not received?'* and *'By the grace of God I am what I am: not I, but the grace of God in me.'* Upon this, as one vanquished, he left me.

"Wherefore I give thanks to my God through Jesus Christ, who has been pleased to give me the victory, and I am persuaded that the tempter shall not again attack me, but, within a short time, I shall, without any great pain of body or anguish of mind, exchange this mortal and miserable life for a blessed immortality through Jesus Christ."

Do you wonder that the devil was eager to have another knock at one who had given so many knocks to his dominion? Do not therefore be at all surprised if Satan rages against you, nor marvel if you yourself should seem to be given into his power. Rather rejoice in this, that his great wrath is the token of the shortness of his time. He wages war with us all the more cruelly because he knows that he will ultimately be defeated. His degraded mind delights in petty malice. If he cannot destroy, he will disturb. If he cannot kill, he will wound.

Subtle as he is, he acts very foolishly in pursuing a hopeless object. In his war against any one of the seed of the woman, he knows that he is doomed to defeat, yet he gnaws at the heel which breaks his head. It is the doom of evil to persevere in its spite after it knows that all is in vain—forever vanquished by the invincible seed of the living God, and yet forever returned to the fray. Sisyphus forever rolling upward a huge stone which returns upon him is a true picture of the devil vainly laboring to remove the truth out of its place. Satan's efforts are indeed *"labor in vain"* (Galatians 4:11 KJV).

I thought this morning that I would call attention to one particular instance of the fact which is seen in the soul that is coming to Christ, for whom Satan often has great wrath knowing that his time is short. My object is to comfort those who are awakened and are seeking the Savior. If they are beset, I desire that they may find peace, rest, and hope very speedily. When the poor man who was possessed with an evil spirit was being brought to Christ, we read that *"as he was still coming, the devil threw him down and convulsed him"* (Luke 9:42). That is the way with the great enemy: when he is about to be cast out, his energy is more displayed than ever, that if possible he may destroy the soul before it has obtained peace with God.

May the sacred Comforter help me while I try to speak encouragingly upon this subject.

Satan Knows His Time Is Short

Our first topic shall be this: how does Satan know when his time is short in a soul? He watches over all souls that are under his power with incessant maliciousness. He goes about the camp like a sentinel, spying out every man who is likely to be a deserter from his army.

In some men's hearts he dwells at ease, like a monarch in his pavilion. Their minds are his favorite mansions. He goes in and out as he pleases and makes himself comfortably at home. He counts the man's nature as his own inheritance and works his own evil pleasure in him. Alas, the deceived man yields his members as instruments of unrighteousness and is willingly held enthralled. All the man's faculties are the many chambers for Satan to dwell in, and his emotions are many fires and forges for Satan to work with.

Eventually, if divine grace interposes, there comes a change. Satan, who has lived there twenty, thirty, forty, fifty, sixty years, begins to think that he shall not be able to keep this residence of his much longer. He perceives that his time is short. I suppose he perceives it first by discovering that he is not quite so welcome as he used to be. The man loved sin and found pleasure in it, but now sin is not so sweet as it was, its flavor is dull and insipid. The charms of vice are fading. Its pleasures are growing empty, vain, and void. This is a token of a great change.

At one time, whenever a pilgrim sin came near, the soul kept open house to entertain it with all hospitality, but now it is not half so eager. Even the indwelling habitual lusts do not yield as much content as before, neither is as much provision made for them. The black prince and his court are out of favor, which is an intimation that he must soon be gone. When sin loses its sweetness, Satan is losing his power. The adversary perceives that he must soon stretch his dragon wings when he sees that the heart is growing weary of him and is breaking away from his fascinations.

He grows more sure of his speedy ejection when he does not get the accommodation he used to have. The man was once eager for sin. He went in the pursuit of vice, hunted after it, and put himself in the way of temptation. Then Satan reigned securely. But now the man begins to forsake the haunts where sin walks openly. He abandons the cups of excitement which inflame the soul. You find him going to a place of worship and listening to a sermon, where before he frequented the taverns and enjoyed a baudy song at a music-hall.

The devil does not like this change and takes it as a warning that he will soon have to give up the key. The man does not drink as once he did, nor swear as once he did, nor does he yield himself up with readiness to every temptation. The fish is getting shy of the bait. The awakened man has not yet decided for Christ, but he is no longer at ease in bondage, no longer the glad slave of iniquity. He is on the wrong road, but he does not run in it. On the contrary, he pauses, heaves a sigh and wishes he could leave the evil road, wishes he knew how to leap a hedge and get into the narrow way. Satan marks all this, and he says to himself, "There is not the

61

preparation made for me that there used to be. There is little readiness to run on my errands. Therefore I perceive that my time is short."

Satan is still more convinced of the shortness of his possession of a man's heart when he hears knocking at that heart's door a hand whose power he has felt. He knows the kind of knock it is: a gentle, but irresistible, knocking upon the heart. Continual, perpetual, persevering is the knock of one who means to enter. The knock is of one that has a hole in His hand. He knocks not as one whose power lies in a blow, but as one whose tears and love are His battery of attack. He has an energy of compassion, an irresistibleness of gentle love. As Satan hears His knock, when he perceives that the tenant of the house hears it too and is half inclined to open the door, he is afraid. When the heart relents at the sound of the Gospel summons, he trembles more. If the knocking still continues, waking up the tenant in the dead of night, a sound heard amid the noise of traffic and above the laughter of fools, he says, "My time is short." He knows the hand which broke his head of old, and its knocking is ominous to him.

He knows that in the gentleness of Jesus there is an irresistible energy which must and will prevail. He therefore counts that his possession of the tenement is precarious when the Gospel is felt in the heart. Between the knocks he hears a voice that says, *"Open for me...for my head is covered with dew, and my locks with the drops of the night!"* (Song of Solomon 5:2), and he knows that this pleading voice bodes the downfall of his power.

Another indication to the enemy that his time is short is when he knows that the tenant of the house steals away sometimes to court and asks for a warrant of eviction against him. You know what I mean—when the man feels that he cannot himself get rid of sin and cannot in his own strength conquer Satan, and therefore cries, "O God, help me. O God, for Christ's sake, drive out the old dragon from my soul, I beseech You." This is asking for a warrant of eviction. This is going to the court of heaven and pleading with the great King to issue a summons and send his officer to eject the intruder, that he may no longer pollute the spirit.

"Ah," says the evil one, "this is not the place for me much longer, for behold he prays." More fierce than the flames of hell to Satan are the prayers of convinced sinners. When they pray he must be gone. He must cry "boot and saddle" when men sound the trumpet of prayer. There is no tarrying in the camp any longer when the advance guard of prayer has come to take possession.

One thing more always makes Satan know that his time is short. That is when the holy Spirit's power is evidently at work within the mind. Light has come in, and the sinner sees and knows what he was ignorant of before. Satan hates the light as much as he loves darkness. Like an owl in the daylight, he feels that he is out of place. Life comes in, too, by the Holy Ghost. The man feels, becomes sensitive, and becomes penitent. Satan, who loves death and ever abides among the tombs, is bound to fly away from life. The Holy Spirit is beginning to work upon the man very graciously. Satan knows every throb of the Spirit's power, for it is the death of his power. So he says, "go to the place from where I came out, for this house trembles as if it were shaken with an earthquake and affords me no rest." Joyful tidings for a heart long molested by this fierce fiend!

Away, enemy, your destructions shall soon come to a perpetual end!

Satan's Display of Rage

Secondly, this brings me to notice that, inasmuch as the shortness of his tenure stirs up the rage of Satan, we must next observe how he displays his great wrath. His fury rages differently in different persons.

On some Satan displays his great wrath by stimulating outward persecution. The man is not a Christian yet, he is not actually converted yet, but Satan is so afraid that he will be saved that he sets all his dogs upon him directly. The poor soul goes into the workshop. Though he would give his eyes if he could say, "I am a Christian," he cannot quite say so. Yet his workmates begin to pounce upon him as much as if he was indeed one of the hated followers of Jesus. They scoff at him because he is serious and sober, because he is beginning to think and to be decent, because he begins to listen to the Gospel and to care for the best things. Before the Christ child was born, the dragon longed to devour

Him. Before a man gets to be a Christian, the prince of the power of the air labors, if possible, to destroy him.

The devil will lose nothing through being behind. He begins as soon as grace begins. Now, if the grace of God is not in the awakened man, and his reformation is only a spasm of remorse, it is very likely that he will be driven back frcm all attendance upon the means of grace by the ribald remarks of the ungodly. However, if the Lord Jesus Christ has really been knocking at his door and the Spirit of God has begun to work, this opposition will not answer its purpose. The Lord will find wings for this poor soul so that he may flee away from the trial which as yet he is not able to bear.

I have sometimes known such opposition even to tend to undo Satan's work and accomplish quite the opposite purpose. I know one who was very troubled about the truth of Scriptures and about the doctrines of the Gospel, although he was a sincere searcher into the truth. He began to attend this house of prayer and to listen to the Gospel, as an enquirer rather than as a believer. As yet he could not state that he was a Christian, though he half wished he could. Now, it came to pass that the opposition which he immediately received from the world strengthened his faith in the Bible and became a sort of missing link between him and the truth. The sneers of his comrades acted in this way. He said to himself, "Why should they all attack me on the bare supposition of my being a Christian? If I had been a Muslim or a Jew, they would have regarded me with curiosity and let me alone. But inasmuch as they only suspect me of becoming a Christian, they are all down upon me with contempt and anger. Now, why is this? Is not this a proof that I am right and that the Word of God is right, for did it not say that there should be enmity between the seed of the serpent and the seed of the woman?"

The devil did not know what he was doing when he opposed that young man and made a believer of him by that which was meant to drive him into unbelief. If the men of this world oppose the faith of our Lord Jesus Christ more fiercely than any other, surely it must be that there is something special in it, something opposed to their sinful ways or to their proud hopes, something which is of God. That was the inference which my young friend drew from the treatment he received, and that inference established him in the faith. Thus, you see, Satan often hopes to save his dominion when his time is short through vehement persecution against the awakening sinner.

Much worse, however, is his other method of showing his wrath, namely, by vomiting floods out of his mouth to drown our new-born hope, if possible. When the hopeful hearer as yet has not really found peace and rest, it will sometimes happen that Satan will try him with doubts, blasphemies, and temptations such as he never knew before. The tempted one has been amazed and has said to himself, "How is this? Can my desire for Christ be the work of God? I get worse and worse. I never felt as wicked as this until I began to seek a Savior." Yet this is no strange thing, fiery though the trial is.

Satan will suggest all the doubts he can about the inspiration of Scripture, the existence of God, the deity of Christ, and everything else that is revealed, till the poor heart that is earnestly longing for salvation will scarcely know whether there is anything true at all. The man will be so jumbled in his thoughts that he will hardly know whether he is on his head or his heels. *"They reel to and fro, and stagger like a drunken man, and are at their wits' end"* (Psalm 107:27). The more they read the Bible and the more they attend to the means of grace, the more they are tempted to be skeptical and atheistic. Doubts they never knew before will torment them even while they strive to be devout. The evil tenant has notice to quit, and he makes up his mind to do all the damage within his power while he is yet within the doors. See how he breaks up precious truths and dashes down the richest hopes, and all with the detestable design of venting his spite upon the poor soul.

At such a time, also, Satan will often arouse all the worst passions of our nature and drive them into unruly riot. The awakened sinner will be astonished as he finds himself beset with temptations more base and foul than he has ever felt before. He will resist and strive against the assault, but it may be so violent it staggers him. He can scarcely believe that the flesh is so utterly corrupt. The man who is anxiously seeking to go to heaven seems at such a time as if he were dragged down by seven strong demons to the eternal depths of perdition. He feels as if he had never known sin before, nor been so completely beneath its power. The satanic troopers sleep as if in a quiet garrison while the man is under the spell of sin, but when once the heart is likely to be captured by Immanuel's love, the infernal soldiery put on their worst manner and trample down all the thoughts and desires of the soul.

Satan may also attack the seeker in another form, with fierce accusations and judgments. He does not accuse some men, for he is quite sure that they are his very good friends. But when a man is likely to be lost to him, he alters his tone and threatens and condemns. He cries, "What, you be saved? It is impossible! You know what you used to be. Think of your past life." Then he rakes up a very hell before the man's eyes. "You!" he accuses, "why even since you have pretended to be a little better and have begun to attend to the means of grace, you know you have looked back with a longing eye and hungered for your old pleasures. It is quite out of the question that you should be a servant of Christ! He will not have such a ragamuffin as you in His house. The great Captain will never march at the head of a regiment which is disgraced by receiving such as you."

Bunyan describes Apollyon as standing across the road and swearing by his infernal den that the pilgrim should go no further. There would he spill his soul. Then he began to fling at him all manner of fiery darts. Among them was this one, "Thou didst faint at first setting out, when thou wast almost choked in the gulf of Despond. Thou wast almost persuaded to go back at the sight of the Lions. Thou hast been false already to thy new Lord!"

Think for a moment of the devil chiding us for sin! Oh, that the poor burdened soul could laugh at this hypocritical accuser, for he hates to be despised and yet he right well deserves it. Laugh at him, O virgin daughter of Zion, for this great wrath of his is because his time is short. Who is he that he should bring an accusation against us? Let him mind himself. He has enough to answer for. When he turns to being an accuser, it is enough to make the child of God laugh him to scorn. Yet it is not easy to laugh when you are in this predicament, for the heart is ready to break with anguish.

Satan at such times has been known to pour into the poor troubled mind floods of blasphemy. I do not recollect as a child having heard blasphemy. Carefully brought up and kept out of harm's way, I think it could only have been once or twice that I ever heard profane language. Yet, when I was seeking the Lord, I distinctly remember the spot where the most hideous blasphemies that ever passed the human mind rushed through my mind. I clapped my hands over my mouth for fear I would utter one of them. They were none of my inventing, neither had I revived them from my memory. They were the immediate suggestions of Satan himself, who was determined, if possible, to drive me to despair.

Read the story of John Bunyan's five years of torture under this particular misery, and you will see how Satan would say to him, "Sell Christ. Sell Christ. Give up Christ." As he went about his daily business, he would have it ringing in his ears, "Sell Christ. Sell Christ." When at last in a moment of torment, Bunyan thought he said, "Let Him go, if He will," then came the accusation, "Now it is all over with you. Jesus will have nothing to do with you, for you have given him up. You are a Judas, you have sold your Lord." Then when the poor man sought the Lord with tears and found peace again, some other dreadful insinuation would dog his heels. John Bunyan was too precious a servant of the devil for him to lose readily. The enemy had perhaps some idea of what kind of servant of God the converted tinker would become, and what sort of dreams would charm the hearts of many generations, so he would not let him go without summoning all the tribes of hell to wreak their vengeance on him if they could not detain him in their service. Yet Bunyan escaped, and so will others in like case.

Oh, bondslave of the devil, may you have grace to steal away to Jesus. Hasten away from Satan's power at once. Otherwise he will, as long as he has any opportunity, manifest his great wrath towards you.

How to Deal with Satan's Attacks

Thirdly, let us think how we are to meet all of this. How must Satan be dealt with while he is showing his great wrath because his power is short?

I should say, first, if he is putting himself in this rage, let us get him out all the more quickly. If he remains quiet, even then we ought to be anxious to be rid of his foul company. But if he shows this great rage, let us get him out straight away. In God's name, let the dragon be smitten if he is raving. If there is any opportunity of getting him out, back door or front door, straight away, do not let us loiter or linger even for a single hour. A devil raging, making us blaspheme, and then accusing us, tempting us, and betraying us, is such a dangerous occupant of a heart that he is not to be borne. Out he must go, and out at once. It is better to have a den of lions dwelling in our house than the devil within our heart.

Lord, turn him out at once by Your own grace. We decide once for all to wage war with him. We will linger no longer: we dare not. We will procrastinate no more. It is more than our lives are worth. Not tomorrow, but today, must the tyrant go. Not after we leave this tabernacle, but here, in this very pew, O Lord, drive the old dragon from his throne with all his hellish crew!

That is the first advice I give you. Let the enemy be cast out at once by grace divine.

The next thing is, inasmuch as we cannot get him out by our own unaided efforts, let us cry to the strong for strength, who can drive out this prince of the power of the air. There is life in a look at Jesus Christ. As soon as that life comes, away goes this prince of darkness as to his domination and reigning power. Oh, soul, there is nothing left for you but to look to Jesus Christ alone. Worried as you are and almost devoured, now is your time to put your trust in Jesus, who is mighty to save.

You know the text in Amos which speaks of the shepherds taking out of the lion's mouth two legs or a piece of an ear. The sheep was almost devoured, but still he pulled out from between the lion's jaws the last relics of his prey. If you seem to be reduced to two legs and a piece of an ear, yet still our glorious Shepherd can pull you out from between the lion's teeth and make you whole again, for He will not lose lost sheep even at its last extremity.

What can you do against Satan? You would with pleasure be rid of him, but what can you do? Do nothing but this: cry to his Master against him. He may be mighty, but set the Almighty One upon him. He who accuses you, refer him to your Advocate. When he brings your sin before you, throw the blood of atonement in his face. Here is a text that will drive him down to his den, *"The blood of Jesus Christ His Son cleanses us from all sin."* (1 John 1:7). Another is, *"This is a faithful saying and worthy of all acceptance, that Christ Jesus came into the world to save sinners, of whom I am chief"* (1 Timothy 1:15). Quit battling with the wily foe. Do not answer the old deceiver. If he tells you you are a blasphemer, admit it. If he says you are utterly lost, own it. Then cast yourself at Jesus' feet, and He will overcome your foe and set you free.

One more comfort for you is this: the more he rages, the more must your poor, troubled heart be encouraged to believe that he will soon be gone. I venture to say that nothing will make him go sooner than your full belief that he has to go. Courageous hope is a weapon which he dreads. Tell him he must soon be gone. He has been accusing you and pouring venom into your mind, making you believe that it is your blasphemy, when it is not yours but his. Say to him, "Ah, but you will be gone soon. You may rage, but you will have to be gone."

"I have full possession of you," he says, "soul and body, and I triumph over you."

Respond to him, "And would you triumph over me as you do if you did not know that you will soon be driven out?"

"Ah," says he, "you will be lost, you will be lost." He howls at you as if ready to devour.

Say to him, "If I was sure to be lost, you would not tell me so, you would sing sweet songs in my ears and lure me to destruction. You have to go, you know you do."

"Oh," says he, "it is impossible you should be saved. You will be damned. You will have the hottest place in hell."

"Yes," say you, "but who sent you to tell me that? You never spoke the truth yet. You are a liar from the beginning, and you are only saying this because you have to go. You know you have to go." Tell him so, and it is not long before he will depart. Say, "Rejoice not over me, O mine enemy; though I fall yet shall I rise again."

Tell him you know his Master. Tell him he may nibble at your heel, but you recall the One that broke his head. Point to his broken head. He always tries to hide it if he can. Tell him his crown is battered to pieces, and tell him where that deed was done and by whose blessed hand.

As you tell him these things, he will shrink back. You shall find yourself alone with Jesus only. Then will Jesus say to you, *"Where are those accusers of yours?"* You will look around and the enemy will be gone. Then your blessed Master will say, *"Neither do I condemn you; go and sin no more"* (John 8:10, 11). The Lord grant us such a riddance of our arch-enemy, and to get it this very moment, for Christ's dear sake. Amen.

3

Satanic Hindrances

Satan hindered us.
—1 Thessalonians 2:18

Paul, Silas, and Timothy were very desirous to visit the church at Thessalonica, but they were unable to do so for the singular reason announced in this text, namely, *"Satan hindered us."* It was not from lack of will, for they had a very great attachment to the Thessalonian brethren, and they longed to look them in the face again. They said of the Thessalonians, *"We give thanks to God always for you all, making mention of you in our prayers,*

*remembering without ceasing your work of
faith, labor of love, and patience of hope in
our Lord Jesus Christ in the sight of our
God and Father"* (1 Thessalonians 1:2-3).
Their will was overruled about visiting the
church together, but being anxious for its
welfare, they sent Timothy alone to minister for a time in its midst. It was not lack
of will which hindered them, but want of
power.

They were not prevented by God's
special providence. We find on certain
occasions that Paul was not allowed to go
precisely where his heart would have led
him. *"They tried to go into Bithynia, but the
Spirit did not permit them"* (Acts 16:7).
*"They were forbidden by the Holy Spirit to
preach the word in Asia"* (Acts 16:6). Rather, their course was directed towards Troas
that they might preach in Europe the
unsearchable riches of Christ.

They could not, however, trace their ab-
sence from Thessalonica to any divine in-
terposition. It appeared to them to proceed
from the great adversary; *"Satan hindered
them."* How Satan did so would be useless
to state dogmatically, but we may form a
reasonable conjecture. I find in the margin
of my pulpit Bible, this note by Bagster,

which may probably be correct: "Satan hindered Paul by raising such a storm of persecution against him at Berea, and other places, that it was deemed prudent to delay his visit till the storm was somewhat allayed."

However, I can hardly surmise this to have been the only hindrance, for Paul was very courageous. Having a strong desire to visit Thessalonica, no fear of opposition would have kept him away. He did not shun the hottest part of the battle, but like a truly valiant champion, delighted most to be found in the thick of his foes. Possibly the antagonism of the various philosophers whom he met with at Athens and the evident heresies at Corinth, from which it seems that this epistle was written, may have called for his presence on the scene of action. He felt that he could not leave struggling churches to their enemies. He must contend with the grievous wolves, and unmask the evil ones who wore the garb of angels of light.

Satan had moved the enemies of the truth to industrious opposition, and thus the apostle and his companions were hindered from going to Thessalonica. It may be that Satan had stirred up dissensions and discords in the churches which Paul was visiting, and therefore he was obliged to stop first in one and then in another to settle their differences, to bring to bear the weight of his own spiritual influence upon the various divided sections of the church to restore them to unity. Well, whether persecution, philosophic heresy, or the divisions in the church were the outward instruments we cannot tell, but Satan was assuredly the prime mover.

You will perhaps wonder why the devil should care so much about Paul and his whereabouts. Why should he take so much interest in keeping these three men from that particular church? This leads us to observe what wonderful importance is attached to the action of Christian ministers. Here was the master of all evil, the prince of the power of the air, intently watching the journeying of three humble men. And he was apparently far more concerned about their movements than about the doings of Nero or Tiberius. These despised heralds of mercy were his most dreaded foes. They preached that name which makes hell tremble. They declared that righteousness against which satanic hate always vents itself with its utmost power. With such malicious glances the arch-enemy watched their daily path. What cunning hands hindered them at all points!

It strikes us that Satan was desirous to keep these apostolic men from the church of Thessalonica because the church was young and weak. Thus, he thought that if it was not fostered and succored by the preaching and presence of Paul, he might yet slay the young child. Moreover, he has from old a fierce hatred of the preaching of the Gospel and possibly there had been no public declaration of the truth throughout Thessalonica since Paul had gone. He was afraid lest the fire-brands of the truth of the Gospel should be again flung in among the masses and a gracious conflagration should take place.

Besides, Satan always hates Christian fellowship. It is his policy to keep Christians apart. Anything which can divide saints from one another, he delights in. He attaches far more importance to godly relationships than we do. Since union is strength, he does his best to promote separation. Just so, he would keep Paul away from these brethren who might have gladdened his heart, and whose hearts he might have cheered. He would hinder their fraternal intimacy that they might miss the strength which always flows from Christian communion and Christian sympathy.

This is not the only occasion in which Satan has hindered good men. Indeed this has been his practice in all ages. We have selected this one particular incident so that some who are hindered by Satan may draw comfort from it, and so that we may have an opportunity (if the Spirit of God shall enable us) of saying a good and forceful word to any who count it strange because this fiery trial has happened unto them.

Satan's Habit of Hindrance

Let us begin this discourse by observing that it has been Satan's practice from old to hinder, wherever he could, the work of God.

"Satan hindered us" is the testimony which all the saints in heaven will bear against the arch-enemy. This is the witness of all who have written a holy line on the historic page or carved a consecrated name on the rock of immortality: *"Satan hindered us."*

In the sacred writings, we find Satan interfering to hinder the completeness of the personal character of individual saints. The man of Uz was perfect and upright before God, and to all appearances would persevere in producing a finished picture of what the believer in God should be. Indeed, Job had so been enabled to live that the arch-fiend could find no fault with his actions, and only dared to impute wrong motives to him. Satan had considered Job, yet he could find no mischief in him. But then he hinted, *"Have You not made a hedge around him, around his household, and around all that he has on every side?"* (Job 1:10).

Satan sought to turn the life-blessing which Job was giving to God into a curse, and therefore he buffeted him severely. He stripped him of all his substance. The evil messengers followed on one another's heels, and their tidings of woe only ceased when his goods were all destroyed and his children had all perished. The poor afflicted parent was then struck in his bone and in his flesh till he was reduced to sit upon a dung hill and scrape himself with a potsherd. Even then the picture had no blot of sin upon it, and the ink pen was held with a steady hand by the patient one. Therefore Satan made another attempt to hinder Job's retaining his holy character. He stirred his wife to say, *"Do you still hold to your integrity? Curse God and die!"* (Job 2:9). This was a great and grievous hindrance to the completion of Job's marvelous career, but, glory be unto God, the man of patience not only overcame Satan, he also made him a stepping-stone to a yet greater height of illustrious virtue. You know about the patience of Job, which you would not have known if Satan had not illuminated it with the blaze of flaming afflictions. Had not the vessel been burnt in the furnace, the bright colors would not have been so fixed and abiding. The trial through which Job passed brought out the lustre of his matchless endurance in submission and resignation to God.

Now, just as the enemy of old waylaid and beset the patriarch to hinder his perseverance in the fair path of excellence, so will he do with us. You may be congratulating yourself this morning, "I have so far walked consistently. No man can challenge my integrity." Beware of boasting, for your virtue will yet be tried. Satan will direct his engines against that very virtue for which you are the most famous. If you have been hitherto a firm believer, your faith will soon be attacked. If up till now you have been meek as Moses, expect to be tempted to speak unadvisedly with your lips. The birds will peck at your ripest fruit, and the wild boar will dash his tusks at your choicest vines. O that we had among us more prominence of piety, more generosity of character, more fidelity of behavior! In all these respects, I doubt not, many have set out with the highest aims and intentions. Alas! How often have they had to cry, *"Satan hindered us!"*

This is not the enemy's only business, for he is very earnest in endeavoring to hinder the emancipation of the Lord's redeemed ones. You know the memorable story of Moses. When the children of Israel were in captivity in Egypt, God's servant stood before their haughty oppressor with his rod in his hand. In Jehovah's name, he declared, *"Thus says the LORD, 'Let My people go, that they may serve Me'"* (Exodus 8:1). A sign was required. The rod was cast upon the ground, and it became a serpent. At this point, Satan hindered. *"Jannes and Jambres resisted Moses"* (2 Timothy 3:8). We read that the magicians did so with their enchantments. Whether by devilish arts or by sleight of hand, we need not now inquire. In either case they did the devil service, and they did it well, for Pharaoh's heart was hardened when he saw that the magicians apparently produced the same miracles as Moses had.

Brethren, take this as a type of Satan's hindrances to the Word of the Lord. Christ's servants came forth to preach the Gospel. Their ministry was attended with signs and wonders. "My kingdom is shaken," said the prince of evil, "I must bestir myself." Straightway he sent magicians to work lying signs and wonders without number. Apocryphal wonders were and are as plentiful as the frogs of Egypt. Did the apostles preach the sacrifice of Christ? The devil's apostles preached the sacrifice of the mass. Did the saints uplift the cross? The devil's servants upheld the crucifix. Did God's ministers speak of Jesus as the one infallible Head of the church? The devil's servants proclaimed the false priest of Rome as standing in that same place. Romanism is a most ingenious imitation of the Gospel. It is the *"magicians [doing] so with their enchantments"* (Exodus 8:7).

If you study well the spirit and genius of the great Antichrist, you will see that its great power lies in its being an exceedingly clever counterfeit of the Gospel of the Lord Jesus Christ. To the extent that tinsel could counterfeit gold, paste could simulate the gem, candlelight could rival the sun in its glory, and a drop in the bucket could imitate the sea in its strength, the spirit of Antichrist has copied God's great masterpiece, the Gospel of our Lord Jesus Christ. To this day, as God's servants scatter the pure gold of truth, their worst enemies are those who utter base coin on which they have feloniously stamped the image and superscription of the lying of kings.

You have another case farther on in history—all Old Testament history is typical of what is going on around us now. God was about to give a most wonderful system of instruction to Israel and to the human race, by way of type and ceremony, in the wilderness. Aaron and his sons were selected to represent the great High Priest of our salvation, the Lord Jesus Christ. In every garment which they wore, there was a symbolic significance. Every vessel of that sanctuary in which they ministered taught a lesson. Every single act of worship, whether it the sprinkling of blood or the burning of incense, was made to teach precious and important truths to the sons of men. What a noble roll was that volume of the book which was unfolded in the wilderness at the foot of Sinai! How God declared Himself and the glory of the coming Messiah in the persons of Aaron and his sons!

What then? With this Satan interfered. Moses and Aaron could say, *"Satan hindered us."* Korah, Dathan, and Abiram arrogantly claimed a right to the priesthood. On a certain day they stood forth with brazen censers in their hands, thrusting themselves impertinently into the office which the Lord had assigned to Aaron and to his sons. The earth opened and swallowed them up alive: this was true prophecy of what shall become of those who thrust themselves into the office of the priesthood where none but Jesus Christ can stand.

You may see the parallel this day. Christ Jesus is the only priest who offers the sacrifice of blood, and he brings that sacrifice no more, for having once offered it he has perfected forever those who are set apart. *"This Man, after he had offered one sacrifice for sins forever, sat down at the right hand of God"* (Hebrews 10:12). Paul, with the strongest force of logic, proved that Christ does not offer a continual sacrifice, but that, having offered it once for all, His work was finished, and He now sits at the right hand of the Father.

This doctrine of a finished atonement and a completed sacrifice seemed likely to overrun the world. It was such a gracious unfolding of the divine mind that Satan could not look upon it without desiring to hinder it. Therefore, look on every hand, and you can see Korah, Dathan, and Abiram in those churches which are branches of the Anglican and the Roman. To this very day, men call themselves "priests" and read prayers from a book in which the catechism states, "Then shall the priest say _____." These arrogate to themselves a priesthood other than that which is common to all the saints. Some of them even claim to offer a daily sacrifice, to celebrate an unbloody sacrifice at the thing which they call an altar. They claim to have power to forgive sin, saying to sick and dying persons, "By authority committed unto me, I absolve you from all your sins." This in England, and this throughout

Europe, is the great hindrance to the propagation of the Gospel—the priestly pretensions of a set of men who are no priests of God, though they may be priests of Baal. Thus the ministers of Jesus are made to cry, *"Satan hinders us."*

Take another instance of satanic hatred. When Joshua had led the tribes across the Jordan, they were to attack the various cities which God had given them for a heritage. From Dan to Beersheba the whole land was to be theirs. After the taking of Jericho—the first contact which they had with the heathen Canaanites—ended in disastrous defeat to the servants of God, *"they fled before the men of Ai"* (Joshua 7:4). Here again you hear the cry, *"Satan hindered us."* Joshua might have gone from city to city exterminating the nations, as they justly deserved to be, but Achan had taken of the accursed thing and hidden it in his tent, therefore no victory could be won by Israel till his theft and sacrilege had been put away.

Beloved, this is symbolic of the Christian church. We might go from victory to victory, our home mission operations might be successful, and our foreign agencies might be crowned with triumph if it were not that we have Achans in the camp at home. When churches have no conversions, it is more than probable that hypocrites concealed among them have turned away the Lord's blessing. You who are inconsistent, who make the profession of religion the means of getting wealth, you who unite yourselves with God's people, but at the same time covet the costly Babylonian garment and the wedge of gold, you are those who cut the sinews of Zion's strength. You prevent the Israel of God from going forth to victory. Little do we know, beloved, how Satan has hindered us.

We, as a church, have had much reason to thank God, but how many more within these walls might have been added to the number of this church if it had not been for the coldness of some, the indifference of others, the inconsistency of a few, and the worldliness of many more? Satan hinders us not merely by direct opposition, but by sending Achans into the midst of our camp.

I will give you one more picture. View the building of Jerusalem after it had been destroyed by the Babylonians. When Ezra and Nehemiah were found building, the devil surely stirred up Sanballat and Tobiah to cast down. There was never a revival of religion without a revival of the old enmity. If ever the church of God is to be built, it will be in troubled times. When God's servants are active, Satan is not without vigilant Myrmidons who seek to counteract their efforts.

The history of the Old Testament church is a history of Satan endeavoring to hinder the work of the Lord. I am sure you will admit it has been the same since the days of the Lord Jesus Christ. When he was on earth Satan hindered Him. He dared to attack Him to His face personally. When that failed, Pharisees, Sadducees, Herodians, and men of all sorts hindered Him. When the apostles began their ministry, Herod and the Jews sought to hinder them. When persecution did not avail, then all sorts of heresies and schisms broke out in the Christian church. Satan still hindered them. A very short time after the taking up of our Lord, the precious sons of Zion, comparable to fine gold, had become like earthen pitchers, the work of the hands of the potter. The glory had departed and the lustre of truth was gone because by false doctrine, lukewarmness, and worldliness, Satan hindered them.

When the reformation dawned, if God raised up a Luther, the devil brought out an Ignatius Loyola to hinder him. Here in England, if God had his Latimers and his Wycliffes, the devil had his Gardiners and Bonners. When in the modern reformation Whitfield and Wesley thundered like the voice of God, there were ordained reprobates found to hinder them, to hold them up to reproach and shame.

Never, since the first hour struck in which goodness came into convict with evil, has it ceased to be true that Satan hindered us. From all points of the compass, all along the line of battle, in the vanguard and in the rear, at the dawn of day and in the midnight, Satan hindered us. If we toil in the field he seeks to break the plowshare. If we build the walls, he labors to cast down the stones. If we would serve God in suffering or in conflict, everywhere Satan hinders us.

Satan's Hindering Tactics

Secondly, we shall now indicate many ways in which Satan has hindered us.

The prince of evil is very busy in hindering those who are just coming to Jesus Christ. Here he spends the main portion of his skill. Some of us who know the Savior recollect the fierce conflicts which we had with Satan when we first looked to the cross and lived.

Others of you, here this morning, are just passing through that trying season. I will address myself to you. Beloved friends, you long to be saved, but ever since you have given any attention to these eternal things, you have been the victim of deep distress of mind. Do not marvel at this. This is usual, so usual as to be almost universal.

I would wonder if you are not perplexed about the doctrine of election. It will be suggested to you that you are not one of the chosen of God, although your common sense will teach you that it might just as well be suggested to you that you are, since you know neither the one nor the other, nor indeed can know until you have believed Jesus. Your present business is with the precept which is revealed, not with election which is concealed. Your business is with that exhortation, *"Believe on the*

Lord Jesus Christ, and you shall be saved" (Acts 16:31).

It is possible that the great fighting ground between predestination and freewill may be the dry and desert place in which your soul is wandering. Now you will never find any comfort there. The wisest of men have despaired of ever solving the mystery of those two matters, and it is not probable that you will find any peace in worrying yourself about it. Your business is not with metaphysical difficulty, but with faith in the atonement of the Lord Jesus Christ, which is simple and plain enough.

It is possible that your sins now come to your remembrance, and though once you thought little enough of them, now it is hinted to you by satanic malice that they are too great to be pardoned. I pray you, reveal the lie of this by telling Satan this truth, that *"every sin and blasphemy will be forgiven men"* (Matthew 12:31).

It is very likely that the sin against the Holy Ghost much torments you. You read that *"anyone who speaks a word against... the Holy Spirit, it will not be forgiven"* (Luke 12:10). In this, too, you may be greatly tried. I wonder not that you are, for this is a most painfully difficult subject.

One fact may cheer you: if you repent of your sins, you have not committed the unpardonable offence, since that sin necessitates hardness of heart forever. So long as a man has any tenderness of conscience and any softness of spirit, he has not so renounced the Holy Spirit as to have lost His presence.

It may be that you are the victim of blasphemous thoughts this very morning, since you have been sitting here. Torrents of the filth of hell have been pouring through your soul. At this, be not astonished, for there are some of us who delight in holiness and are pure in heart, who nevertheless have been at times sorely tried with thoughts which were never born in our hearts, but which were injected into them. These suggestions are born in hell, not in our spirits. They are hated and loathed but are cast into our minds to hinder and trouble us.

Now though, Satan may hinder you as he did the child who was brought to Jesus. We read about him that as he *was still coming, the demon threw him down and convulsed him*" (Luke 9:42). Do come notwithstanding. Though seven demons were in him, Jesus would not cast the coming sinner out. Even though you should feel a conviction that the unpardonable sin has fallen to your lot, yet dare to trust in Jesus. If you do that, I warrant you there shall be a joy and a peace in believing which shall overcome him of whom we read, that he has *"hindered us."*

But I must not stop long on any one point when there are so many. Satan is sure to hinder Christians when they are earnest in prayer. Have you not frequently found, dear friends, when you have been most earnest in supplication, that something or other will dart across your mind to make you cease from the exercise? It appears to me that we shake the tree and no fruit drops from it. Just when one more shake would bring down the luscious fruit, the devil touches us on the shoulder and tells us it is time to be gone, and so we miss the blessing we might have attained. I mean that just when prayer would be the most successful, we are tempted to abstain from it. When my spirit has sometimes laid hold upon the angel, I have been painfully conscious of a counter-influence urging me to cease from such petition and let the Lord alone, for His will would be done. If the temptation did not come in that shape, yet

99

it came in another, to cease to pray because prayer after all could not avail. O brethren, I know if you are much in prayer you can sing Cowper's hymn:

"That various hindrances we meet
In coming to the mercy seat."

The same is true of Christians when under the prompting of the Spirit of God or when planning any good work. You may have been prompted sometimes to speak to someone. "Run, speak to that young man" has been the message in your ear. You have not done it: Satan has hindered you. You have been told on a certain occasion—you do not know how, but believe me we ought to pay great respect to these inward whispers—to visit a certain person and help him. You have not done it: Satan hindered you. You have been sitting down by the fire one evening reading a missionary report concerning Afghanistan or some district destitute of the truth. You have thought, "Now I have a little money which I might give to this purpose." Then it has come across your mind that there is another way of spending it more profitably for your family: so Satan has hindered you. Or you yourself thought of doing a little in a certain district by way of preaching and teaching or some other form of Christian effort. As sure as you began to plan it, something or other arose, and Satan hindered you. If he possibly can, he will come upon God's people in those times when they are full of thought and ardor and ready for Christian effort, that he may murder their infant plans and cast these suggestions of the Holy Spirit out of their minds.

How often too has Satan hindered us when we have entered into the work! In fact, beloved, we never ought to expect a success unless we hear the devil making a noise. I have taken it as a certain sign that I am doing little good when the devil is quiet. It is generally a sign that Christ's kingdom is coming when men begin to lie against you and slander you and the world is in an uproar, casting about your name as evil.

Oh, those blessed tempests! Do not give me calm weather when the air is still and heavy and when lethargy is creeping over one's spirit. Lord, send a hurricane. Give us a little stormy weather. When the lightning flashes and the thunder rolls, then God's servants know that the Lord is abroad, that His right hand is no longer kept in His bosom, that the moral atmosphere will get clear, that God's kingdom will come and His will shall be done on earth, even as it is in heaven.

"Peace, peace, peace," is the flap of the dragon's wings. The stern voice which proclaims perpetual war is the voice of the Captain of our salvation. You say, how is this? *Do not think that I came to bring peace on earth. I did not come to bring peace but a sword. For I have come to set a man against his father, a daughter against her mother, and the daughter-in-law against her mother-inlaw. And a man's foes will be those of his own household"* (Matthew 10:34-36). Christ does make physical peace. There is to be no strife with the fist, no blow with the sword. But moral and spiritual peace can never exist in this world where Jesus Christ is, as long as error is there.

You know, beloved, that you cannot do any good thing, but the devil will be sure to hinder you. What then? Up and at him! Coward looks and faint counsels are not for warriors of the cross. Expect fighting and you will not be disappointed. Whitfield used to say that some ministers would go from the first of January to the end of December with a perfectly whole skin. The devil never thought them worth attacking. But let us begin to preach with all our might and soul and strength the Gospel of Jesus Christ, and men will soon put a fool's cap on our heads and begin laughing at us, ridiculing us. If so, so much the better. We are not alarmed because Satan hinders us.

Nor will he only hinder us in working. He will hinder us in seeking to unite with one another. We are about to make an effort, as Christian churches in London, to come closer together, and I am happy to find indications of success. But I should not wonder but what Satan will hinder us, and I would ask your prayers that Satan may be routed in this matter and that the union of our churches may be accomplished. As a church ourselves, we have walked together in peace for a long time, but I should not marvel if Satan would try to thrust in the cloven foot to hinder our walking in love, peace, and unity.

Satan will hinder us in our communion with Jesus Christ. When at his table, we think to ourselves, "I shall have a sweet moment now," just then vanity intrudes.

Like Abraham, you offer the sacrifice, but the unclean birds come down upon it, and you need to drive them away. *"Satan hindered us."* He is not omnipresent, but by his numerous servants he works in all kinds of places and manages to distract the saints when they would serve the Lord.

Rules for Discernment

In the third place there are two or three rules by which these hindrances may be detected as satanic.

I think I heard somebody saying to himself this morning, "Yes, I should have risen in the world, and have been a man of money now if it had not been that Satan hindered me." Do not believe it, dear friend. I do not believe that Satan generally hinders people from getting rich. He would just as soon that they should be rich as poor. He delights to see God's servants set upon the pinnacle of the temple, for he knows the position to be dangerous. High places and God's praise do seldom well agree. If you hare been hindered in growing rich, I should rather set that down to the good providence of God which would not place you where you could not have borne the temptation.

"Yes," said another, "I had intended to have lived in a certain district and done well, but have not been able to go. Perhaps that is the devil." Perhaps it was. Perhaps it was not. God's providence will know best where to place us. We are not always choosers of our own locality. We are not always to conclude when we are hindered and disappointed in our own intentions that Satan has done it, for it may very often be the good providence of God.

But how may I tell when Satan hinders me? I think you may tell thus: first, by the purpose. Satan's object in hindering us is to prevent our glorifying God. If anything has happened to you which has prevented your growing holy, useful, humble, and sanctified, then you may trace that to Satan. If the distinct object of the interference to the general current of your life has been that you may be turned from righteousness to sin, then from the objective you may guess the author. It is not God who does this, but Satan. Yet know that God does sometimes put apparent hindrances in the way of his own people, even in regard to their usefulness and growth in grace. But His objective is still to be considered: it is to try his saints and so to strengthen them. The purpose of Satan is to turn them out of the right road and make them take the crooked way.

You may tell the suggestions of Satan, again, by the method in which they come: God employs good motives, Satan bad ones. If what has turned your attention away from your the Lord has been a bad thought, a bad doctrine, a bad teaching, a bad motive—that never came from God, that must be from Satan.

Again, you may tell the suggestions from their nature. Whenever an impediment to usefulness is pleasing or gratifying to you, consider that it came from Satan. Satan never brushes the feathers of his birds the wrong way. He generally deals with us according to our tastes and likings. He flavors his bait to his fish. He knows exactly how to deal with each man, and to put that motive which will fall in with the suggestions of the carnal nature. Now, if the difficulty in your way is rather contrary to yourself than for yourself, then it comes from God. If that which now is a hindrance brings you gain, pleasure, or advantage in any way, rest assured it came from Satan.

We can tell the suggestions of Satan, once more, by their season. Hindrances to prayer, for instance, if they are satanic, come out of the natural course and relation of human thoughts. It is a law of the mind that one thought suggests another, which suggests the next, and so on, as the links of a chain are one after theother. But satanic temptations do not come in the regular order of thinking: they dash upon the mind unawares. My soul is in prayer, so it would be unnatural that I should then blaspheme, yet then the blasphemy comes. Therefore it is clearly satanic and not from my own mind. If I am set upon doing my Master's will but a cowardly thought assails me, that idea which differs from the natural run of my mind and thoughts may be at once ejected as not being mine, and may be set down to the account of the devil who is the true father of it.

By these means I think we may tell when Satan hinders, and when it is our own heart, or when it is of God. We ought carefully to watch that we do not put the saddle on the wrong horse. Do not blame the devil when it is yourself. On the other hand, when the Lord puts a bar in your way, do not attribute this to Satan, and so go against the providence of God. It may be difficult at times to see the way of duty, but if you go to the throne of God in prayer you will soon discover it. *"Bring the ephod here"* (1 Samuel 23:7), said David when he was in difficulty. Do you say the same? Go to the great High Priest, whose business it is to give forth the oracle! Lo, upon His breast hangs the Urim and Thummim, and you shall from Him find direction in every time of difficulty and dilemma.

Acting against Hindrances

Supposing that we have ascertained that hindrances in our way really come from Satan, what do we do then? I have but one piece of advice, and that is to go on, hindrance or no hindrance, in the path of duty as God the Holy Ghost enables you.

If Satan hinders you, I have already hinted that this opposition should cheer you. "I did not expect," said a Christian minister, "to be easy in this particular pastorate, or else I would not have come here. I always count it," said he, "to be my duty to show the devil that I am his enemy, and if I do that, I expect that he will show me that he is mine." If you are now opposed and you can trace that opposition distinctly to Satan, congratulate yourself upon it. Do not sit down and fret. Why, it is a great thing that a poor creature like you can actually vex the great prince of darkness and win his hate. It makes the race of man the more noble when it comes in conflict with a race of spirits and stands toe to toe even with the prince of darkness himself.

It is a dreadful thing, doubtless, that you should be hindered by such an adversary, but it is most hopeful, for if he were your friend, you might have cause to fear indeed. Stand out against him, because you have now an opportunity of making a greater gain than you could have had if he been quiet. You could never have had a victory over him if you had not engaged in conflict with him. The poor saint would go on his inglorious way to heaven if he were untempted, but being tormented, every step of his pathway becomes glorious. Our position today is like that described by

Bunyan, when from the top of the palace the song was heard:

"Come in, come in,
Eternal glory thou shalt win."

Now merely to ascend the stairs of the palace, though safe work, would not have been very ennobling. However, when the foes crowded round the door blocking every stair, the hero came to the man with the ink stand, who sat before the door, and said, "Write my name down, sir." Then to get from the lowest step to the top where the bright ones were singing made every inch glorious. If devils did not oppose my path from earth to heaven, I might travel joyously, peacefully, safely, but certainly without renown. But now, when every step is contested in winning our pathway to glory, every single step is covered with immortal fame. Press on then, Christian. The more opposition, the more honor.

Be in earnest against these hindrances when you consider, again, what you lose if you do not resist him and overcome him. To allow Satan to overcome me would be eternal ruin to my soul. Certainly it would forever blast all hopes of my usefulness. If

I retreat and turn my back in the day of battle, what will the rest of God's servants say? What shouts of derision would ring over the battlefield! How the banner of the covenant would be trailed in the mire! Why, we must not, we dare not, play the coward. We dare not give way to the insinuation of Satan and turn from the Master, for the defeat would then be too dreadful to be endured.

Beloved, let me feed your courage with the recollection that your Lord and Master has overcome. See Him there before you. He of the crown of thorns has fought the enemy and broken his head. Satan has been completely vanquished by the Captain of your salvation. That victory was representative—He fought and won it for you.

You have to contend with a defeated foe, and one who knows and feels his disgrace. Though he may fight with desperation, yet he fights not with true courage, for be is hopeless of ultimate victory. Strike, then, for Christ has smitten him. Down with him, for Jesus has had him under his foot. You, weakest of all the host, triumph, for the Captain has triumphed before you.

Lastly, remember that you have a promise to help you gird up your loins and play the man this day. *"Resist the devil, and he will flee from you"* (James 4:7). Christian minister, do not resign your situation. Do not think of sending in your resignation because the church is divided and the enemy is making headway. Resist the devil. Flee not, but make him flee. Christian young men, you who have begun to preach in the street, or distribute tracts, or visit frown house to house, though Satan hinders you very much, I pray you now redouble your efforts. It is because Satan is afraid of you that he resists you, because he would rob you of the great blessing which is now descending on your head. Resist him, and stand fast. You Christian pleading in prayer, do not let go your hold upon the covenant angel now. For now that Satan hinders you, it is because the blessing is descending. You are seeking Christ, so close not those eyes or turn not away your face from Calvary's streaming tree. Now that Satan hinders you, it is because the night is almost over and the day star begins to shine. Brethren, you who are most tormented, most sorrowfully tried, most borne down, yours is the brighter hope. Be now courageous. Play the man for God, for Christ, for your own soul. The day shall come when you with your Master shall ride triumphant through the streets of the New Jerusalem with sin, death, and hell captive at your chariot wheels, and you with your Lord crowned as victor, having overcome through the blood of the Lamb.

May God bless you, dear friends now present. I do not know to whom this sermon may be most suitable, but I believe it is sent especially to certain tried saints. The Lord enable them to find comfort in it. Amen.

4

Christ, the Conqueror of Satan

*And I will put enmity
between you and the woman,
and between your seed and her Seed;
He shall bruise your head,
and you shall bruise His heel.*
—Genesis 3:16

This is the first gospel sermon that was ever delivered upon the surface of this earth. It was a memorable discourse indeed, with Jehovah himself for the preacher, and the whole human race and the prince of darkness for the audience. It must be worthy of our heartiest attention.

Is it not remarkable that this great gospel promise should have been delivered so soon after the transgression? As yet no sentence had been pronounced upon either of the two human offenders, but the promise was given under the form of a sentence pronounced upon the serpent. Not yet had the woman been condemned to painful travail, or the man to exhausting labor, or even the soil to the curse of thorn and thistle. Truly *"mercy triumphs over judgment"* (James 2:13). Before the Lord had said *"Dust you are, and to dust you shall return"* (Genesis 3:19), He was pleased to say that the seed of the woman should bruise the serpent's head. Let us rejoice, then, in the swift mercy of God which, in the early watches of the night of sin, came with comforting words to us.

These words were not directly spoken to Adam and Eve, but they were directed distinctly to the serpent himself, and that by way of punishment to him for what he had done. It was a day of cruel triumph to him. Such joy as his dark mind is capable of had filled him, for he had indulged his malice, and gratified his spite. He had in the worst sense destroyed a part of God's works. He had introduced sin into the new world, had stamped the human race with his own image, and had gained new forces to promote rebellion and to multiply transgression. Therefore, he felt that sort of gladness which a fiend can know who bears a hell within him.

But now God comes in, takes up the quarrel personally, and causes him to be disgraced on the very battlefield upon which he had gained a temporary success. He tells the dragon that He will undertake to deal with him; this quarrel shall not be between the serpent and man, but between God and the serpent. God says, in solemn words, *"I will put enmity between you and the woman, between your seed and her Seed."* He promises that there shall rise in fullness of time a champion, who, though He may suffer, shall smite in a vital part the power of evil by bruising the serpent's head. It seems to me that this was the more comforting message of mercy to Adam and Eve, because they could feel sure that the tempter would be punished, and as that punishment would involve blessing for them, the vengeance due to the serpent would be the guarantee of mercy to themselves.

Perhaps, however, by thus obliquely giving the promise, the Lord meant to say, "Not for your sakes do I this, fallen man and woman, nor for the sake of your descendants. Rather for My own name and honor's sake, that it be not profaned and blasphemed among the fallen spirits. I undertake to repair the mischief which has been caused by the tempter, that My name and My glory may not be diminished among the immortal spirits who look down upon the scene." All this would be very humbling but yet consolatory to our parents if they thought of it, seeing that mercy given for God's sake is always to our troubled apprehension more sure than any favor which could be promised to us for our own sakes. The divine sovereignty and glory afford us a stronger foundation of hope than merit, even if merit could be supposed to exist.

Now we must note concerning this first gospel sermon that on it the earliest believers steadied themselves. This was all that Adam had by way of revelation, and all that Abel had received. This one lone star shone in Abel's sky; he looked up to it and believed. By its light he spelled out "sacrifice," and thus he brought of the firstlings of his flock and laid them upon the altar. He proved in his own person how the seed of the serpent hated the seed of the woman, for his brother killed him for his testimony. Although Enoch, the seventh from Adam, prophesied concerning the second advent, yet he does not appear to have uttered anything new concerning the first coming, so that still this one promise remained as man's sole word of hope. The torch which flamed within the gates of Eden just before man was driven forth lit up the world to all believers until the Lord was pleased to give more light, and to renew and enlarge the revelation of his covenant, when He spoke to his servant Noah.

Those silvery-haired fathers who lived before the flood rejoiced in the mysterious language of our text. Resting on it, they died in faith. Nor, brethren, must you think it a slender revelation, for it is wonderfully full of meaning if you attentively consider it. If it had been on my heart to handle it doctrinally this morning, I think I could have shown you that it contains the whole gospel. There lie within it, as an oak lies within an acorn, all the great truths which make up the Gospel of Christ.

Observe that here is the grand mystery of the incarnation. Christ is that seed of the woman who is here spoken of. There is a broad hint as to how that incarnation would be effected. Jesus was not born after the ordinary manner of the sons of men. Mary was overshadowed by the Holy Ghost, and *"that Holy One"* (Luke 1:35) which was born of her was, concerning His humanity, the seed of the woman only. As it is written, *"Behold, the virgin shall conceive and bear a Son, and shall call His name Immanuel"* (Isaiah 7:14). The promise plainly teaches that the Deliverer would be born of a woman. Viewed carefully, it also foreshadows the divine method of the Redeemer's conception and birth.

So also is the doctrine of the two seeds plainly taught here: *"I will put enmity between you and the woman, between your seed and her Seed."* There was evidently to be in the world a seed of the woman on God's side against the serpent, and a seed of the serpent that should always be upon the evil side, even as it is unto this day. The church of God and the temple of Satan both exist. We see an Abel and a Cain, an

Isaac and an Ishmael, a Jacob and an Esau. Those that are born after the flesh are the children of their father the devil, for his works they do. But those that are born-again, being born of the Spirit after the power of the life of Christ, are thus in Christ Jesus the seed of the woman, and contend earnestly against the dragon and his seed.

Here, too, the great fact of the sufferings of Christ is foretold clearly: *"You shall bruise His heel."* Within those words we find the whole story of our Lord's sorrows from Bethlehem to Calvary.

"He shall bruise your head." Here is the breaking of Satan's regal power; here is the clearing away of sin; here is the destruction of death by resurrection; here is the leading of captivity captive in the ascension; here is the victory of truth in the world through the descent of the Spirit; here is the latter-day glory in which Satan shall be bound; and lastly, here is the casting of the evil one and all his followers into the lake of fire. The conflict and the conquest are both encompassed by these few fruitful words.

The words may not have been fully understood by those who first heard them, but to us they are now full of light. The text at first looks like a flint, hard and cold; but sparks fly from it plentifully, for hidden fires of infinite love and grace lie concealed within. Over this promise of a gracious God, we ought to rejoice exceedingly.

We do not know what our first parents understood by it, but we may be certain that they gathered a great amount of comfort from it. They must have understood that they were not then and there to be destroyed, because the Lord had spoken of a *"Seed."* They could reason that it must be that Eve would live if there should be a seed from her. They understood, too, that if that seed was to overcome the serpent and bruise his head, it must herald good to themselves: they could not fail to see that there was some great, mysterious benefit to be conferred upon them by the victory which their seed would achieve over the instigator of their ruin. They continued on in faith upon this, and were comforted in travail and in toil. I do not doubt that both Adam and his wife in this faith entered into everlasting rest.

This morning I intend to handle this text in three ways. First, we shall notice it's facts. Secondly, we shall consider the experience within the heart of each believer which tallies to those facts. Thirdly, we shall find the encouragement which the text and its connection as a whole afford to us.

The Facts

The facts are four, and I call your earnest attention to them. The first is that enmity was stirred up. The text begins, *"I will put enmity between you and the woman."* They had been very friendly. The woman and the serpent had conversed together. She thought at the time that the serpent was her friend. She was so much his friend that she took his advice in the face of God's precept and was willing to believe bad things of the great Creator, because this wicked, crafty serpent insinuated the same. Now, at the moment when God spoke, that friendship between the woman and the serpent had already in a measure come to an end, for she had accused the serpent to God by saying, *"The serpent deceived me, and I ate"* (Genesis

3:13). So far, so good. The friendship of sinners does not last long; they have already begun to quarrel, and now the Lord comes in and graciously takes advantage of the quarrel which had commenced, and says, "I will carry this disagreement a great deal further. I will put enmity between the serpent and the woman."

Satan counted on man's descendants being his confederates, but God would break up this covenant with hell and raise up a Seed which would war against the satanic power. Thus we have here God's first declaration that He would set up a rival kingdom to oppose the tyranny of sin and Satan, that He will create in the hearts of a chosen seed an enmity against evil so that they shall fight against it, and with many a struggle and pain shall overcome the prince of darkness. The divine Spirit has abundantly achieved this plan and purpose of the Lord, combating the fallen angel by a glorious man, and making man to be Satan's foe and conqueror.

Henceforth, the woman was to hate the evil one, and I do not doubt but that she did so. She had abundant cause for so doing. As often as she thought of him, it would be with infinite regret that she could have listened to his malicious and deceitful talk. The woman's seed has also evermore had enmity against the evil one. I mean not the carnal seed, for Paul tells us, *"Those who are the children of the flesh, these are not the children of God; but the children of the promise are counted as the seed"* (Romans 9:8). The carnal seed of the man and the woman are not meant, but rather the spiritual seed, even Christ Jesus and those who are in Him. Wherever you meet these, they hate the serpent with a perfect hatred. We would if we could destroy from our souls every work of Satan, and out of this poor afflicted world of ours we would root up every evil which he has planted.

That glorious Seed of the woman—for He speaks not of many seeds, but of one Seed—you know how he abhorred the devil and all his devices. There was enmity between Christ and Satan, for he came to destroy the works of the devil and to deliver those who are under bondage to him. For that purpose was He born; for that purpose did He live; for that purpose did He die; for that purpose He has gone into glory; and for that purpose He will come again, that everywhere He may root out

His adversary and utterly destroy him and his works from among the sons of men.

This putting of the enmity between the two seeds was the commencement of the plan of mercy, the first act in the program of grace. Of the woman's seed it was henceforth said, *"You love righteousness and hate wickedness; therefore God, Your God, has anointed You with the oil of gladness more than Your companions"* (Psalm 45:7).

The second prophecy, which has also turned into a fact, concerns the coming of the Champion. The Seed of the woman by promise is to champion the cause and oppose the dragon. That Seed is the Lord Jesus Christ. The prophet Micah says, *"But you, Bethlehem Ephrathah, though you are little among the thousands of Judah, yet out of you shall come forth to Me the One to be ruler in Israel, Whose goings forth have been from of old, from everlasting. Therefore He shall give them up, until the time that she who is in labor has given birth"* (Micah 5:2-3). To none other than the Babe which was born in Bethlehem of the blessed virgin can these words of prophecy refer. She it was who conceived and bore a Son. Concerning her Son we sing, *"For unto us a Child is born, unto us a Son is given; and the government shall be upon His shoulder. And His name shall be called Wonderful, Counselor, Mighty God, Everlasting Father, the Prince of Peace"* (Isaiah 9:6). One memorable night at Bethlehem, when angels sang in heaven, the Seed of the woman appeared. As soon as He saw the light, the old serpent, the devil, planted into the heart of Herod the desire to slay Him, but the Father preserved Him and allowed none to lay hands on Him.

As soon as Jesus publicly came forward upon the stage of action, thirty years later, Satan met Him toe to toe. You know the story of the temptation in the wilderness, and how there the woman's Seed fought with him who was a liar from the beginning. The devil assailed Him three times with all the artillery of flattery, malice, craft, and falsehood, but the peerless Champion stood unwounded, and chased His foe from the field. Then our Lord set up his kingdom, called one and another unto Himself, and carried the war into the enemy's country. In many places He cast out devils. He spoke to the wicked, unclean spirit, *"You deaf and dumb spirit, I command you, come out of him,"* and the demon was expelled. Legions of devils flew before Him: they sought to hide themselves in swine to escape from the terror of His presence. *"Have You come here to torment us before the time?"* (Matthew 8:29) was their cry when the wonder-working Christ dislodged them from the bodies which they tormented. Yes, He made His own disciples mighty against the evil one, for in His name they cast out devils, till Jesus said, *"I saw Satan fall like lightning from heaven"* (Luke 10:18).

Then there came a second personal conflict, for I take it that Gethsemane's sorrows were to a great degree caused by a personal assault of Satan, for our Master said, *"This is your hour, and the power of darkness"* (Luke 22:53). He said also, *"The ruler of this world is coming, and he has nothing in Me"* (John 14:30). What a struggle it was.

Though Satan had nothing in Christ, yet he sought if possible to lead him away from completing his great sacrifice. There our Master's *"sweat became like great drops of blood falling down to the ground"* (Luke 22:44) in the agony which it cost Him to contend with the fiend. Then it was that our Champion began the last fight of all and won it to the bruising of the serpent's head. Nor did He end until He had spoiled principalities and powers and made a show of them openly.

> "Now is the hour of darkness past,
> Christ has assumed his reigning power;
> Behold the great accuser cast
> Down from his seat to reign no more."

The conflict of our glorious Lord continues in His seed. We preach Christ crucified, and every sermon shakes the gates of hell. We bring sinners to Jesus by the Spirit's power, and every convert is a stone torn down from the wall of Satan's mighty castle. Yes, the day shall come when everywhere the evil one shall be overcome, and the words of John in Revelation shall be fulfilled:

> *So the great dragon was cast out, that serpent of old, called the Devil and Satan, which deceives the whole world...*
> *Then I heard a loud voice saying in heaven, "Now salvation, and strength, and the kingdom of our God, and the power of His Christhave come, for the accuser of our brethren who accused them before our God day and night, has been cast down."*
> *(Revelation 12:9-10)*

Thus did the Lord God in the words of our text promise a Champion who should be the Seed of the woman, between whom and Satan there should be war forever and ever. That Champion has come, and the manchild has been born. Though the dragon is raging with the woman and makes war with the remnant of her seed which keep the testimony of Jesus Christ, yet the battle is the Lord's, and the victory falls unto Him whose name is *"Faithful and True, and [who] in righteousness judges and makes war"* (Revelation 19:11).

The third fact which comes out in the text, though not quite in that order, is that our Champion's heel should be bruised. Do you need me to explain this? You know how all through His life His heel—that is, His lower part, His human nature—was perpetually being made to suffer. He carried our sicknesses and sorrows. But the bruising came mainly when, both in body and in mind, His whole human nature was made to agonize when His soul was exceeding sorrowful even unto death, and His enemies pierced His hands and His feet, and He endured the shame and pain of death by crucifixion.

Look at your Master and your King upon the cross, all stained with blood and dust! There was His heel most cruelly bruised. When they took down that precious body and wrapped it in fair white linen and in spices, and laid it in Joseph's tomb, they wept as they handled that casket in which the Deity had dwelt, for there again Satan had bruised His heel. It was not merely that God had bruised Him, *"yet it pleased the Lord to bruise Him"* (Isaiah 53:10). But the devil had let loose Herod, Pilate, Caiaphas, the Jews, and the Romans—all of them his tools—upon Him whom he knew to be the Christ, so that He was bruised of the old serpent.

That is all, however! It was only His heel, not His head, which was bruised! The Champion rose again. The bruise was not mortal nor continual. Though He died, yet still so brief is the interval in which He slumbered in the tomb that His holy body had not seen corruption, and He came forth perfect and lovely in His manhood, rising from His grave as from a refreshing sleep after so long a day of unresting toil! Oh, the triumph of that hour! As Jacob only limped with his injured hip when he overcame the angel, so Jesus just retained a scar in His heel, and that He bears to the skies as His glory and beauty. Before the throne He looks like a lamb that has been slain, but in the power of an endless life He lives unto God.

Then comes the fourth fact, namely, that while His heel was being bruised, He was to bruise the serpent's head. The figure represents the dragon as inflicting an injury upon the Champion's heel, but at the same moment the Champion Himself with that heel crushes in the head of the serpent with fatal effect. By His sufferings Christ has overthrown Satan, by the heel that was bruised He has trodden upon the head which devised the bruising.

> Lo, by the sons of hell he dies;
> But as he hangs 'twixt earth and skies,
> He gives their prince a fatal blow,
> And triumphs o'er the powers below.

Though Satan is not dead, my brethren, I was about to say, I would to God that he were. Though he is not converted, and never will be, nor will the malice of his heart ever be driven from him, yet Christ has so far broken his head that he has missed his mark altogether. He intended to make the human race the captives of his power, but they are redeemed from his iron yoke. God has delivered many of them, and the day shall come when He will cleanse the whole earth from the serpent's slimy trail, so that the entire world shall be full of the praises of God.

Satan thought that this world would be the arena of his victory over God and good. Instead, it is already the grandest theater of divine wisdom, love, grace, and power. Heaven itself is not so resplendent with mercy as the earth is, for here it is the Savior poured out His blood.

No doubt, he thought that when he had led our race astray and brought death upon us, he had effectually marred the Lord's work. He rejoiced that we would all pass under the cold seal of death, and that our bodies would rot in the sepulcher. Had he not spoiled the handiwork of his great Lord? God may make man as a curious creature with intertwisted veins and nerves, sinews and muscles, and He may put into his nostrils the breath of life; but, "Ah," says Satan, "I have infused a poison into him which will make him return to the dust from which he was taken."

But now, behold, our Champion whose heel was bruised has risen from the dead and given us a pledge that all His followers shall rise from the dead also. Thus Satan was foiled, for death shall not retain a bone, nor a piece of a bone, of one of those who belonged to the woman's seed. At the trump of the archangel from the earth and from the sea we shall arise, and this shall be our shout, *"O Death, where is your sting? O Hades, where is your victory?"* (1 Corinthians 15:55). Satan, knowing this, feels already that by the resurrection his head is broken. Glory be to the Christ of God for this!

In multitudes of other ways, the devil has been vanquished by our Lord Jesus, and so shall he ever be until he is cast into the lake of fire.

Comparing Our Experiences

Let us now view our experience as it tallies with these facts. Now, brothers and sisters, we were by nature, as many of us as have been saved, the heirs of wrath even as others. It does not matter how godly our parents were, the first birth brought us no spiritual life, for the promise is to them *"who were born, not of blood, nor of the will of the flesh, nor of the will of man, but [only to those who are born] of God"* (John 1:13). *"That which is born of the flesh is flesh"* (John 3:6); you cannot make it anything else and there it abides. The flesh, or carnal mind, abides in death; it is not reconciled to God, neither indeed can it be. He who is born into this world but once, and knows nothing of the new birth, must place himself among the seed of the serpent, for only by regeneration can we know ourselves to be the true seed.

How does God deal with us who are His called and chosen ones? He means to save us, and how does he work to that end? The first thing he does is that He comes to us in mercy and puts enmity between us and the serpent. That is the very first work of grace. There was peace between us and Satan once. When he tempted, we yielded. Whatever he taught us, we believed. We were his willing slaves.

But perhaps you, my brethren, can recall when you first began to feel uneasy and dissatisfied. The world's pleasures no longer pleased you. All the juice seemed to have been taken out of the apple, and you had nothing left but the hard core which you could not feed upon at all. Then you suddenly perceived that you were living in sin, and you were miserable about it. Though you could not get rid of sin, yet you hated it, sighed over it, and cried and groaned. In your heart of hearts you remained no longer on the side of evil, for you began to cry, *"O wretched man that I am! Who will deliver me from this body of death?"* (Romans 7:24).

You were already from of old in the covenant of grace ordained to be the woman's seed, and now the decree began to discover itself in life bestowed upon you and working in you. The Lord in infinite mercy dropped the divine life into your soul. You did not know it, but there it was, a spark of the celestial fire, the living and incorruptible seed which abides forever. You began to hate sin, and you groaned under it as under a galling yoke. More and more it burdened you, you could not bear it, and you hated the very thought of it.

So it was with you. Is it so now? Is there still enmity between you and the serpent? Indeed you are more and more the sworn enemies of evil, and you willingly acknowledge it.

Then came the Champion: that is to say, *"Christ in you, the hope of glory"* (Colossians 1:27) was formed. You heard of Him and understood the truth about Him. It seemed a wonderful thing that He should be your substitute and stand in your room and place and stead, that He should bear your sin and all its curse and punishment, and that He should give his righteousness and His very self to you that you might be saved. Ah, then you saw how sin could be overthrown, did you not? As soon as your heart understood Christ, then you saw that what the law could not do, in that it was weak through the flesh, Christ was able to accomplish. You understood that the power of sin and Satan under which you had been in bondage, and which you now loathed, could and would be broken and destroyed because Christ had come into the world to overcome it.

Next, do you recollect how you were led to see the bruising of Christ's heel and to stand in wonder and observe what the enmity of the serpent had worked in Him? Did you not begin to feel the bruised heel yourself? Did not sin torment you? Did not

137

the very thought of it vex you? Did not your own heart become a plague to you? Did not Satan begin to tempt you? Did he not inject blasphemous thoughts and urge you on to desperate measures? Did he not teach you to doubt the existence of God, and the mercy of God, and the possibility of your salvation, and so on? This was his nibbling at your heel. He is up to his old tricks still. He bothers whom he can't devour with a malicious joy.

Did not your worldly friends begin to annoy you? Did they not give you the cold shoulder because they saw something about you so strange and foreign to their tastes? Did they not impute your conduct to fanaticism, pride, obstinacy, bigotry, and the like? Ah, this persecution is the serpent's seed beginning to discover the woman's seed, and to carry on the old war. What does Paul say? *"But as he who was born according to the flesh then persecuted him who was born according to the Spirit, even so it is now"* (Galatians 4:29). True godliness is an unnatural and strange thing to them, and they cannot do away with it. Though there are no stakes in Smithfield, nor racks in the Tower, yet the enmity of the human heart towards Christ and his seed is just the same, and very often shows itself in *"trial of mockings"* (Hebrews 11:36) which to tender hearts are very hard to bear. Well, this is your heel being bruised in sympathy with the bruising of the heel of the glorious Seed of the woman.

But, brethren, do you know something of the other fact, that we conquer because the serpent's head is broken in us? How do you say? Is not the power and dominion of sin broken in you? Do you not feel that you cannot sin because you are born of God? Some sins which were masters of you once do not trouble you now. I have known a man guilty of profane swearing, and from the moment of his conversion, he has never had any difficulty in the matter. We have known a man snatched from drunkenness, and the cure by divine grace has been very wonderful and complete. We have known persons delivered from unclean living, and they have at once become chaste and pure, because Christ has smitten the old dragon such blows that he could not have power over them in that respect. The chosen seed sin and mourn it, but they are not slaves to sin; their heart goes not after it. They have to say sometimes *"the evil I will not to do, that I practice"* (Romans 7:19), but they are wretched if they do. With their hearts they consent to the law of God that it is good. They sigh and cry that they may be helped to obey it, for they are no longer under the slavery of sin. The serpent's reigning power and dominion is broken in them.

It is broken next in this way, that the guilt of sin is gone. The great power of the serpent lies in unpardoned sin. He cries, "I have made you guilty. I brought you under the curse."

"No," say we, "we are delivered from the curse and are now blessed, for it is written, *'Blessed is he whose transgression is forgiven, whose sin is covered'* (Psalm 32:1). We are no longer guilty, for who shall lay anything to the charge of God's elect? Since Christ has justified, who is he that condemns?" Here is a swinging blow for the old dragon's head, from which he will never recover.

Oftentimes the Lord also grants us to know what it is to overcome temptation, and so to break the head of the fiend. Satan allures us with many baits. He has studied our points well; he knows the weakness of the flesh. But many times, blessed be God, we have completely foiled him to his eternal shame! The devil must have felt himself small that day when he tried to overthrow Job, dragged him down to a dung hill, robbed him of everything, covered him with sores, and yet could not make him yield. Job conquered when he cried, *"Through He slay me, yet will I trust Him."* (Job 13:15). A feeble man had vanquished a devil who could raise the wind and blow down a house, and destroy the family who were feasting in it. Devil as he is, and crowned prince of the power of the air, yet the poor bereaved patriarch sitting on the dung hill covered with sores, being one of the woman's seed, through the strength of the inner life won the victory over him.

> "Ye sons of God oppose his rage,
> Resist, and he'll be gone:
> Thus did our dearest Lord engage
> And vanquish him alone."

Moreover, dear brethren, we have this hope that the very being of sin in us will be destroyed. The day will come when we shall be without spot or wrinkle, or any such thing; and we shall stand before the throne of God, having suffered no injury whatever from the fall and from all the machinations of Satan, for *"they are without fault before the throne of God"* (Revelation 14:5). What triumph that will be! *"The God of peace will crush Satan under your feet shortly"* (Romans 16:20). When He has made you perfect and free from all sin, as He will do, you will have bruised the serpent's head indeed. And your resurrection, too, when Satan shall see you come up from the grave like one that has been perfumed in a bath of spices, and when he shall see you arise in the image of Christ —with the same body which was sown in corruption and weakness, now raised in incorruption and power—then will he feel an infinite chagrin and know that his head is bruised by the woman's seed.

I ought to add that every time any one of us is made useful in saving souls, we repeat the bruising of the serpent's head. When you go, dear sister, among those poor children and pick them up from the gutters, where they are Satan's prey, where he finds the raw material for thieves and criminals, and when through your means, by the grace of God, the little wanderers become children of the living God, then you in your measure bruise the old serpent's head. I pray you do not spare him. When we, by preaching the Gospel, turn sinners from the error of their ways so that they escape from the power of darkness, again we bruise the serpent's head. Whenever in any shape or way you are blessed to the aiding of the cause of truth and righteousness in the world, you, too, who were once beneath his power, and even now have sometimes to suffer from his nibbling at your heel, you tread upon his head. In all deliverances and victories, you overcome and prove the promise true, *"You shall tread upon the lion and the cobra, the young lion and the serpent you shall trample under foot. Because he has set his love upon Me, therefore will I deliver him; I will set him on high, because he has known My name"* (Psalm 91:13-14).

Encouragement

Let us speak awhile upon the encouragement which our text and the context yields to us, for it seems to me to abound. I want you, brethren, to exercise faith in the promise and be comforted.

The text evidently encouraged Adam very much. I do not think we have attached enough importance to the conduct of Adam after the Lord had spoken to him. Notice the simple but conclusive proof which he gave of his faith. Sometimes an action may be very small and unimportant, and yet, as a straw shows which way the wind blows, it may display at once, if it be thought over, the whole state of the man's mind.

Adam acted in faith upon what God said, for we read, *"And Adam called his wife's name Eve [or Life], because she was the mother of all living"* (Genesis 3:20). She was not a mother at all, but as the life was to come through her by virtue of the promised seed, Adam marks his full conviction of the truth of the promise though at the time the woman had borne no children.

There stood Adam, fresh from the awful presence of God. What more could he say? He might have said with the prophet, *"My flesh trembles for fear of You"* (Psalm 119:120), but even then he turns round to his fellow-culprit as she stands there trembling too, and calls her Eve, mother of the life that is yet to be. It was grandly spoken by father Adam: it makes him rise in our esteem. Had he been left to himself, he would have murmured or at least despaired, but no, his faith in the new promise gave him hope. He uttered no deploring word against the condemnation to till with toil the unthankful ground, nor on Eve's part was there a word of lament over the appointed sorrows of motherhood. They each accept the well-deserved sentence with the silence which denotes the perfection of their resignation. Their only word is full of simple faith. There was no child on whom to set their hopes, nor would the true seed be born for many an age, yet Eve is to be the mother of all living, and Adam calls her so.

Exercise the same kind of faith, my brother, on the far wider revelation which God has given to you, and always extract the utmost comfort from it. Make it a point, whenever you receive a promise from God, to get all you can out of it. If you carry out that rule, it is wonderful what comfort you will gain. Some go on the principle of getting as little as possible out of God's word. I believe that such a plan is the proper way with a man's word; always understand it at the minimum, because that is what he means. But God's word is to be understood at the maximum, for He will do exceeding abundantly above what you ask or even think.

Notice by way of further encouragement that we may regard our reception of Christ's righteousness as an installment of the final overthrow of the devil. *"Also for Adam and his wife the Lord God made tunics of skins, and clothed them"* (Genesis 3:21). A very condescending, thoughtful, and instructive deed of divine love! God heard what Adam said to his wife and saw that he was a believer. So He comes and gives him the type of the perfect righteousness which is the believer's portion. He covered him with lasting raiment. No more fig leaves, which were a mere mockery, but a close-fitting garment which had been procured through the death of a victim. The Lord brings that and puts it on him, and Adam could no more say, "I am naked." How could he, for God had clothed him?

Now, beloved, let us take out of the promise that is given us concerning our Lord's conquest over the devil this one item and rejoice in it. Christ has delivered us from the power of the serpent, who opened our eyes and told us we were naked. By covering us from head to foot with righteousness which adorns and protects us, He makes us comfortable in heart and beautiful in the sight of God, and we are no more ashamed.

Next, by way of encouragement in pursuing the Christian life, I would say to young people, expect to be assailed. If you have fallen into trouble through being a Christian, be encouraged by it. Do not at all regret or fear it, but rejoice in that day and leap for joy, for this is the constant token of the covenant. There is enmity between the Seed of the woman and the seed of the serpent still. If you did not experience any of it, you might begin to fear that you were on the wrong side. Now that you smart under the sneer of sarcasm and oppression, rejoice and triumph, for now are you partakers with the glorious Seed of the woman in the bruising of His heel.

Still further encouragement comes from this. Your suffering as a Christian is not brought upon you for your own sake; you are partners with the great Seed of the woman and are confederates with Christ. You must not think the devil cares much about you: the battle is against Christ in you. Why, if you were not in Christ, the devil would never trouble you. When you were without Christ in the world, you might have sinned as you liked. Your relatives and workmates would not have been at all grieved with you, and they would rather have joined you in it. But now the serpent's seed hates Christ in you. This exalts the sufferings of persecution to a position far above all common afflictions.

I have heard of a woman who was condemned to death in the Marian days. Before her time came to be burned, a child was born to her, and she cried out in her pain. A wicked adversary, who stood by said, "How will you bear to die for your religion if you make such ado?"

"Ah," she said, "Now I suffer in my own person as a woman, but then I shall not suffer, but Christ in me." Nor were these idle words, for she bore her martyrdom with exemplary patience and rose in her chariot of fire in holy triumph to heaven. If Christ be in you, nothing will dismay you, but you will overcome the world, the flesh, and the devil by faith.

Last of all, let us always resist the devil with this belief, that he has received a broken head. I am inclined to think that Luther's way of laughing at the devil was a very good one, for he is worthy of shame and everlasting contempt. Luther once threw an ink stand at his head when he was tempting him very sorely. Though the act itself appears absurd enough, yet it was a true type of what that greater reformer was all his life long. The books he wrote were truly a flinging of the ink stand at the head of the fiend.

That is what we have to do. We are to resist him by all means. Let us do this bravely, and tell him to his face that we are not afraid of him. Tell him to recollect his bruised head, which he tries to cover with a crown of pride, or with a clerical cowl, or with an infidel doctor's hood. We know him and see the deadly wound he bears. His power is gone; he is fighting a lost battle; he is contending against omnipotence. He has set himself against the oath of the Father, against the blood of the incarnate Son, and against the eternal power of the blessed Spirit—all of which are engaged in the defense of the Seed of the woman in the day of battle. Therefore, brethren, be steadfast in resisting the evil one, being strong in faith, giving glory to God.

"'Tis by thy blood, immortal Lamb,
Thine armies tread the tempter down;
'Tis by thy word and powerful name
They gain the battle and renown.

"Rejoice ye heavens; let every star
Shine with new glories round the sky:
Saints, while ye sing the heavenly war,
Raise your Deliverer's name on high."

5

Satan Departing, Angels Ministering

*And when the devil had ended all the
temptation, he departed from him
for a season.*
—Luke 4:13 KJV

*Then the devil left Him, and behold,
angels came and ministered to Him.*
—Matthew 4:11

Beloved friends, we have very much to
learn from our Lord's temptation. He
was tempted in all points, like as we are. If
you will study the temptation of Christ,
you will not be ignorant of Satan's devices.
If you see how he defeated the enemy, you

will learn what weapons to use against your great adversary. If you see how our Lord conquers throughout the whole battle, you will learn that, as you keep close to him, you will be *"more than conquerors through Him that loved us"* (Romans 8:37).

From our Lord's temptation, we learn, especially, to pray, *"Lead us not into temptation"* (Matthew 6:13 KJV). Let us never mistake the meaning of that petition. We are to pray that we may not be tempted, for we are poor flesh and blood, and very frail. It is for us to cry to God, *"Lead us not into temptation."*

But we also learn a great deal from the close of our Lord's great threefold trial. We find him afterwards peaceful, ministered unto by angels, and rejoicing. That should teach us to pray, "But, if we must be tempted, *'deliver us from evil'* " (Matthew 6:13 KJV), or, as some render it very correctly, *"Deliver us from the evil one"* (NKJV).

First, we pray that we may not be tempted at all; and then, as a supplement to that prayer, yielding the whole matter to divine wisdom, "But if it is necessary for our personal growth in grace, for the verification of our graces, and for God's glory that we should be tempted, Lord,

152

deliver us from the evil, and especially deliver us from the personification of evil, the evil one!"

With that as an introduction, for a short time tonight let me call upon you to notice in our text, first, the devil leaving the tempted One: *"Then the devil left him."* Secondly, we shall keep to Matthew and notice the angels ministering to the tempted One after the fallen angel had left Him. Then, thirdly, we will mark the limitation of the rest which we may expect, the limitation of the time in which Satan will be gone, as Luke puts it, *"When the devil had ended all the temptation, he departed from him for a season."* Some express it, *"until an opportune time"* (NKJV), when he would again return, and our great Lord and Master would once more be tried by his wicked wiles.

The Devil Leaving

First, we have as the subject for our happy consideration, the devil leaving the tempted One. When did the devil depart from our Lord? When he had finished the temptation. It must have been a great relief to our divine Master when Satan left Him. The very air must have been purer and more fit to be breathed. His soul must have felt a great relief when the evil spirit had gone away.

However, we are told he did not go until he had finished all the temptation. So Luke puts it: *"When the devil had ended all the temptation, he departed from him for a season."* Satan will not go till he has shot the last arrow from his quiver. Such is his malice that, as long as he can tempt, he will tempt. His will desires our total destruction, but his power is not equal to his will. God does not give him power such as he would like to possess. There is always a limit set to his assaults. When Satan has tempted you thoroughly and ended all his temptation, then he will leave you. Since you have not yet undergone all forms of temptation, so you may not expect absolutely and altogether to be left by the arch-enemy. It may be a long time of your suffering from his attacks before he will stay his hand, for he will try all that he possibly can to lead you into evil and to destroy the grace that is in you.

Still, he does come to an end with his temptations sooner than he desires. Just as God has said to the mighty sea, *"This far you may come, but no farther, and here your proud waves must stop"* (Job 38:11), so says He to the devil. When he permitted Satan to try the graces of Job and to prove his sincerity, he let him go just so far, but no farther. When he asked for a further stretch of power, still there was a limit. There is always a limit to Satan's power. When he reaches that point, he will be pulled up short because he can do no more.

You are never so in the hand of Satan as to be out of the hand of God. You are never so tempted, if you are a believer, that there is not a way of escape for you. God permits you to be tried for many reasons which perhaps you could not altogether understand, but which His infinite wisdom understands for you. But He will not suffer the rod of the wicked to rest upon the lot of the righteous. It may fall there, but it shall not stay there. The Lord may let you be put into the fire, but the fire shall be heated no hotter than you are able to bear. *"When the devil had ended all the temptation, he departed from him."*

Satan did not depart from Christ, however, until he had also failed in every temptation. When the Lord had foiled him at every point, had met every temptation with a text of Holy Scripture, and had proved His own determination to hold fast His integrity and not let it go, then the enemy departed. Oh, brothers and sisters, if you can hold out, if you can stand against this and then against that, if you are proof against frowns and proof against flatteries, if you are proof against prosperity and proof against adversity, if you are proof against sly insinuations and open attacks, then the enemy will depart from you! You will have won the day by God's grace, even as your Master did.

"Well," says one, "I wish that he would depart from me, for I have been sorely troubled by him." To this I say most heartily, "Amen."

Let us think, for a minute or two, about when Satan will depart from the child of God, as he did from the great Son of God. I have no doubt that he will do that when he finds that it is necessary for him to be somewhere else. Satan is not everywhere, and cannot be, for he is not divine. He is not omnipresent. But, as someone has said,

156

although he is not everywhere present, it would be hard to say where he is not, for he moves so swiftly and is such an agile spirit that he seems to be here and there and everywhere. Also, where he is not in person, he is represented by that vast host, the legions of fallen spirits, who are under his control. And even where they are not, he carries out his evil devices by leaving the leaven to work and the evil seeds to grow, when he himself has gone elsewhere.

Quite probably, not many times in one's life is any man called into conflict with Satan himself personally. There are too many of us now for him to give all his time and strength to any one. He has to be somewhere else. Oh, I long to be the means of multiplying the number of God's people by the preaching of the Word, that the Gospel of the grace of God may fly abroad and bring in myriads, that the devil may have more to do and therefore not be able to give so much of his furious attention, as he goes in one direction and then another, to individual children of God.

He also leaves God's people very quickly when he sees that they are sustained by superior grace. He hopes to catch them when grace is at a low ebb. If he can come upon them when faith is very weak, when hope's eyes are dim, when love has grown cold, then he thinks that he will make an easy capture. But where we are filled with the Spirit as the Master was (God grant that we may be), he looks us up and down, and he presently veers off. Like an old pirate who hangs about on the lookout for merchant vessels, when he meets with ships that have plenty of guns on board and hardy hands to give him a warm reception, he goes after some other craft not quite so well able to resist his assaults.

Oh, brothers and sisters, do not be mere Christians or only barely Christians with just enough grace to let you see your imperfections. But pray to God to give you mighty grace, that you may *be strong in the Lord and in the power of His might*" (Ephesians 6:10). Then, after the devil has tested you and found that the Lord is with you and that God dwells in you, you may expect that, as it was with your Master, so it will be with you: Satan will leave you.

Sometimes I think, however, that Satan personally leaves us because he knows that, for some men, not to be tempted is a greater danger than to be tempted. "Oh!" say you, "how can that be?" Brothers, sisters, do you know nothing of carnal security, of being left—as you think—to grow in grace and to be very calm, very happy, very useful, and to find beneath you a sea of glass with not a ripple on the waves? You say, "Yes, I do know that experience and have been thankful for it."

Have you never found creeping over you, at the same time, the idea that you are somebody, that you are getting wonderfully experienced, that you are an important child of God, rich and increased in goods? And have you not held, like David, *"Now in my prosperity I said, 'I shall never be moved'"* (Psalm 30:6)?

Possibly you have looked askance on some of your friends, who have been trembling and timid, crying to God from day to day to keep them. You have been Sir Mighty, Lord Great-One, and everybody should bow down before you. Ah, yes, you have now fallen into a worse condition than even those are in who are tempted of Satan! A calm in the tropics is more to be dreaded than a tempest. In such a calm everything gets to be still and stagnant. The ship scarcely moves. It is like a painted ship on a painted sea, and it gets to be in something like the state described by Coleridge's *Ancient Mariner*:

> "The very deep did rot:
> Alas, that ever this should be!
> And slimy things with legs did crawl
> Over the slimy sea."

"Oh!" say you, "that is horrible." Yes, and that is the tendency of a soul that is at peace with itself, and is not emptied from vessel to vessel. I fear that is often the case with those who believe themselves to be supernaturally holy.

A curious fact can be proved by abundant evidence, namely, that the boast of human perfection is closely followed by obscenity and licentiousness. The most unclean sects that have ever defaced the page of history have been founded by those who had the notion that they were beyond temptation, that they had ceased to sin and never could transgress again.

"Ah!" says Satan, "this notion does my work a great deal better than tempting a man. When I tempt him, then he stands up to resist me. He has his eyes open, he grasps his sword, and puts on his helmet, he cries to God, 'Lord, help me!' as he watches night and day. The more tempted he is, the more he looks to God for strength. But if I leave him quite alone, and he goes to sleep, then he is not in the battle. If he begins to feel quite secure, then I can steal in upon him unawares, and make a speedy end of him." This is one reason why Satan leaves some men untempted. A roaring devil is better than a sleeping devil. There is no temptation much worse than that of never being tempted at all.

Again, I not doubt that Satan leaves us—for I know that he must—when the Lord says to him what he said in the wilderness, *"Away with you, Satan"* (Matthew 4:10). The Lord does say that when He sees one of his poor children dragged about, tortured, wounded, and bleeding. He says, *"'Away with you, Satan.'* I permit you to fetch in My stray sheep, but not to worry them to death. *'Away with you, Satan.'* "* The old hell-dog knows his Master, and he flies at once.

This voice of God will come when the Lord sees that we cast ourselves wholly upon Him. In my brother's prayer he suggested to us, if you remember, that in casting our burden upon the Lord, we might not be able to get rid of it. The way was to cast ourselves and our burden both upon the Lord. The best way of all is to get rid of the burden entirely, to cast yourself without your burden upon the Lord.

Let me remind you of a story that I once told you, of a gentleman who, riding along in his rig, saw a man carrying a heavy pack and asked him if he would like a ride. "Yes, and thank you, sir." But he kept his pack on his back while riding. When the gentleman asked why he did not take his pack off and set it down, the packman replied, "Why, sir, it is so kind of you to give me a ride that I do not like to impose upon your good nature, and I thought that I would carry the pack myself."

"Well," said the other, "you see, it makes no difference to me whether you carry it or do not carry it, for I am carrying you and your pack. You might as well unstrap it and set it down."

Just so, friend, when you cast your burden upon God, unstrap it. Why should you carry it yourself when God is prepared to bear it? Beloved, there are times when we forget that, but when we can come and absolutely yield ourselves, saying, "Lord, here I am—tempted, poor, and weak—but

I come and rest in You. I know not what to ask at Your hands, but Your servant has said in Psalm 55:22, *'Cast your burden on the LORD, and He shall sustain you; He shall never permit the righteous to be moved.'* I lie at Your feet, my Lord. Here I am, here would I be. Do with me as seems good in Your sight, only deal in tender mercy with Your servant." Then will the Lord rebuke the enemy. The waves of the sea will be still, and there will come a great calm.

So much for the devil leaving the one who is tempted. He does so, he must do so, when God commands it.

Ministering Angels

Secondly, let us think of the angels ministering to the tempted One. The angels came and ministered to our Lord after Satan was gone.

Notice that they did not come while our Lord was in the battle. Why not? Because it was necessary that He should tread the winepress alone, and because it was more glorious for Him that there should be no one with Him! Had there been any angels there to help Him in the duel with the adversary, they might have shared the honor of the victory. But they were stopped till the fight was over. When the foe was gone, then the angels came.

It has been noted that Scripture does not say that the angels came very often and ministered to Jesus, which makes us think that they were always near, that they hovered within earshot, watching and ready to interpose if they might. They were a bodyguard round about our Lord, even as they are today about His people. *"Are they not all ministering spirits sent forth to minister for those who will inherit salvation"* (Hebrews 1:14)?

The moment that the fight was over, then the angels came and ministered to Christ. Why was that? First, I suppose, because, as a man, He was especially exhausted. We are told He was hungry, which shows exhaustion. Besides that, the strain of forty days' temptation must have been immense. Men can bear up under stress, but when it eases, then they fall. Elijah did marvels, smote the priests of Baal, and behaved like a hero. But after it was all over, Elijah failed. As man, our

Lord was subject to the sinless infirmities of our flesh. Thus it was needed that angels should come and minister to Him, even as the angel did in the garden after the agony and bloody sweat.

It was also because, being man, He was to partake of the ministry which God had allotted to man. God has appointed angels to watch over His own people. Inasmuch as Jesus is our Brother, and as God's children are partakers of the ministry of angels, He Himself also shared in the same. Thus, He showed how He took our weaknesses upon Himself, and therefore needed and received that succor which the Father has promised to all of His children.

Also, was it not because He was so beloved of the angels, and they were so loyal to Him? They must have wondered when they saw Him born on earth and living here in poverty. When they saw Him tempted of the enemy, they must have loathed the adversary. How could Satan be permitted to come so near their pure and holy Master?

I think that Milton could have best pictured this scene. He would have described every seraphim there as longing to let his sword of flame find a scabbard in the heart of the foul fiend that dared to come so near to the Prince of purity. But they could not interfere. However, as soon as they were permitted, then they joyfully came and ministered unto Him.

And does it not also go to show that His was a nature very sensitive to the angelic touch? You and I are hard-hearted and coarse.

"Myriads of spirits throng the air:
They are about us now."

Women are to cover their heads in worship *because of the angels* (1 Corinthians 11:10). There are many acts of decorum in holy worship that are to be kept up *because of the angels.* The angels are innumerable and are sent to minister to us, but we are not aware of them—often we do not perceive them. But Jesus was all tenderness and sensitiveness. He knew that the angels were there, so it was easy for them to come and minister to Him. What they did in ministering to Him, we cannot tell. I should certainly think that they sustained His bodily nature, for he hungered, and they readily brought food to Him. But they also sustained His mental and His spiritual nature with words of comfort. The sight of them reminded Him of His Father's house, reminded Him of the glory which He had laid aside. The sight of them proved that the Father did not forget Him, because He had sent the household troops of heaven to succor and support His Son. The sight of them must have made Him anticipate the day of which the poet sings:

"They brought his chariot from above,
To bear him to his throne,
Clapp'd their triumphant wings, and cried,
'The glorious work is done.'"

Now, brethren, if we are tempted, shall we have any angels to succor us? Well, we shall have the equivalent of angels, certainly. Oftentimes, after a temptation, God sends His human messengers. Many of you can tell how, when you have been hearing the Word after a bad time of temptation, the gospel message has been wonderfully sweet to you. You have sat in your pew, and said, "God sent that sermon on purpose for me." Or, if you have not had a sermon, you have read the Bible, and the words have seemed to burn and glow on the page, warming your soul by their heat.

Has it not been so with you often? Are not all the holy things more sweet after trial than they were before? Have you not found them so? I bear my willing witness that never does Christ seem so precious, never do the promises seem so rich and rare, never does evangelical doctrine cling so closely to my heart, and my heart to it, as after a time of painful trial when I have been laid aside from holy service and racked with anguish. Oh, then the angels come and minister to us, in the form of men who preach the Word, or in the form of the living page of God's written Word!

I have noticed, too, that God sometimes cheers his tempted people with clear sunshine after rain by some very gracious providence. Something happens that they could not have looked for, so pleasant, so altogether helpful, that they have had to burst into singing, though just before they had been sighing. The cage door was set wide open, and God's bird had such a flight. It sang so sweetly as it mounted up to heaven's gate that the soul seemed transformed into a holy lark in its ascending music. Have not you found the Lord very gracious to you after some severe trial or some strong temptation? I believe that this is or will be the testimony of many experienced Christians.

As there come these choice providences, so, I do not doubt, there come actual angels ministering to us, though we are unaware of their presence. They can suggest holy thoughts to bring us comfort. But, above the angels, far superior to angelic help is the Holy Ghost, the Comforter. How sweetly can He bind up every wound and make it even sing as it heals! He makes the bones that God had broken to rejoice, and fills us with a deeper experience of delight than we have ever known before.

Well now, I suppose that some of you here tonight are in this condition. Satan has left you, and angels are ministering to you. If so, you are very happy. Bless God for it. There is a great calm. Thank God for the calm after the storm. I hope, my brother that you are the stronger for what you have endured, and that the conflict has matured you, and prepared you for something better.

Now, what did our Lord do after the devil had left him, and the angels had come to minister to him? Did He go home and stop there, and begin to sing of his delightful experiences? No, we find Him preaching directly afterwards, full of the Spirit of God. He went everywhere, proclaiming the kingdom. He was found in the synagogue or on the hillside. Just in proportion as the Spirit of God had enabled Him to overcome the enemy, we find Him going forth to spend that strength in the service of His Father.

O tempted one, have you been granted a respite? Spend that respite for Him who gave it to you. Is it calm now after a storm? Go now, and sow your fields with the good seed. Have you wiped your eyes, and are your salty tears gone? Go, sing a psalm unto your Beloved. Go down to His vineyard, take the foxes, prune the vines and dig about them. Do necessary work for Him who has done so much for you.

Listen. You have been set free. There are many under bondage to Satan—not free as you are—fighting against him, but still his willing slaves. Oh, come, my brother, God has set you free, so go after them! Go after the fallen woman and the drunken man. Go, seek, and find the most debauched, the most depraved. Specially look after any of your own household who have played the prodigal.

"Oh, come, let us go and find them!
In the paths of death they roam:
At the close of the day
'Twill be sweet to say
'I have brought some lost one home.' "

And it will be right to say it, if the Lord
has dealt so well with you.

Limitations on Rest

Now, I have to close by reminding you
of the third point, which is a searching
truth, namely, the limitation of our rest.

Satan left Christ *"for a season,"* or
"until an opportune time." Did the devil
assail our Lord again? I am sure that he
personally did; but he did so in many ways
by others also.

I notice that, before long, he tried to
entangle Him in His speech. That is a very
easy thing to do with us. Somebody tonight
can take up something that I have said,
twist it from its context, and make it sound
and seem totally different from what was
meant by it. You know how the Herodians,
the Sadducees, and the Pharisees did this
with our Lord. They tried to entrap Jesus

171

with His words. In all that, Satan led them on. Satan also actively opposed Christ's ministry, and Christ opposed Satan. But Jesus won the day, for he saw Satan fall like lightning from heaven.

A stil more artful plan was that by which the devil's servants, the demons that were cast out of possessed persons, called Jesus the Son of God. He rebuked them because he did not want any testimony from them. No doubt the devil thought it a very cunning thing to praise the Savior, because then the Savior's friends would begin to be suspicious of Him, if He was praised by the devil. This was a deep trick, but the Master made him hold his tongue. You remember how He commanded on one occasion, *"Be quiet, and come out of him"* (Mark 1:25). It was something like this, "Down dog! Come out!" Christ was never very polite with Satan. A few words and very strong ones are all that are necessary for this arch-prince of wickedness.

Satan tempted our Lord through Peter. That is a plan that he has often tried with us, setting a friend of ours to do his dirty work. Peter took his Lord and rebuked Him when He spoke about being spit upon and put to death. Then the Lord said, *"Get behind me, Satan!"* (Mark 8:33). He could see the devil using Peter's tenderness to try to divert Him from His self-sacrifice. Oh, how often has Satan tempted us that way, entangling us in our speech, opposing us in our work, praising us out of wicked motives to try to deceive us, and then setting some friend to try to direct us from holy self-denial!

There were also occasions when our hearts sink in our Lord. Thus we read in John 12:27, *"Now My soul is troubled, and what shall I say? Father, save Me from this hour."* He seems to have been very heavy in heart at that time. But the deepest sinking of soul was when, in the garden, He cried, *"My soul is exceedingly sorrowful, even to death"* (Matthew 26:38). Satan had a hand in that sore trial, for the Lord had said, *"The ruler of this world is coming"* (John 14:30). He said to those who came to arrest him, *"This is your hour, and the power of darkness"* (Luke 22:53). It was a dreadful season. Our Lord's ministry began and ended with a fierce onslaught from Satan. He left Him after the temptation, but only for a season.

Well now, dear friends, if we have peace and quietness tonight, and are not tempted, do not let us become self-secure. The devil will come to us again at a fit opportunity. And when will that be? There are a great many opportunities with you and with me. One is when we have nothing to do. You know Dr. Watt's lines:

> "Satan finds some mischief still,
> For idle hands to do."

He will come and attack us when we are alone—I mean, when we are sad and lonely, sitting still and moping by ourselves.

But Satan also finds a very fit occasion when we are in company, especially when it is very mixed company, a company of persons who are perhaps superior to ourselves in education and in station, but who do not fear God. We may easily be overawed and led astray by them. Satan will come then.

I have known him frequently to find an occasion against the children of God when we are sick and ill, the old coward! He knows that we would not mind him when we are in good health; but sometimes when we are down in the dumps through sickness and pain, then it is that he begins to tempt us to despair.

So will he do with us when we are very poor. When a man has had a great loss in business, down comes Satan, and insinuates, "Is this how God treats His children? God's people are no better off than other people."

Then, if we are getting on in the world, he turns it the other way and says, " *Does Job fear God for nothing*' (Job 1:9)? He gets ahead by his religion." You cannot please the devil anyhow, and you should not want to please him. He can make a temptation for you out of anything.

I am going to say something that will surprise you. One time of great temptation is when we are very spiritual. As to myself, I have never been in such supreme danger as when I have led some holy meeting with sacred fervor, and have felt carried away with delight in God. You know that it is easy to be atop the Mount of Transfiguration, and then to meet Satan at the foot, as our Lord did when He came down from that hill.

Another time of temptation is when we have already done wrong. "Now he begins to slip," says Satan. "I saw him trip; now I will get him down completely." Oh, for speedy repentance and an earnest flight to Christ, whenever there has been a grave fault, and also before the grave fault comes that we may be preserved from falling!

Satan finds a good occasion for tempting us when we have not sinned. After we have been tempted, and we have won the day and stood fast, then he comes and says, "Now, that was well done on your part. You are a splendid saint." You may depend upon it that he who thinks of himself as a splendid saint is next door to a shameful sinner. Satan soon gets the advantage over him.

If you are successful in business or successful in holy work, then Satan will tempt you. If you are not successful and have had a bad time, then Satan will tempt you. When you have a heavy load to carry, he will tempt you. When that load is taken off, then he will tempt you worse that ever. He will tempt you when you have obtained some blessing that you have been thinking was such a great boon. For example, in the wilderness, when they cried for meat and insisted that they must have it, God gave them their heart's desire, but sent leanness into their souls. Just as you have secured the thing that you are seeking, then comes a temptation. To all of which I say, "Watch." "What I say unto you, I say unto all," said Christ, *"Watch and pray, lest you enter into temptation"* (Matthew 26:41). And by the conflict and the victory of your Master, go into the conflict bravely, expecting to conquer by faith in Him, even as He overcame.

But what shall I say to those who are the slaves and the friends of Satan? The Lord have mercy upon you! If you desire to escape, there is only one way. There is the cross, and Christ hangs upon it. Look to Jesus: He can set you free. He came on purpose to proclaim liberty to the captives. Look and live. Look now, and live now. I implore you, do it, for His dear sake. Amen.

Sprugeon's Exposition of Luke 4:1—16

> *¹Then Jesus being full of the Holy Spirit returned from Jordan, and was led by the Spirit into the wilderness.*

"Full of the Holy Spirit," and then led *"into the wilderness"* to be tempted. You

would not expect that. Yet it is a sadder thing to be led into a wilderness when you are not filled with the Spirit, and a sadder thing to be tempted when the Spirit of God is not resting upon you. The temptation of our Lord was not one to which He wantonly exposed Himself. He *"was led by the Spirit into the wilderness."* The Spirit of God may lead us where we shall have to endure trial. If He does so, we are safe and shall come off conquerors even as our Master did.

²Being tempted for forty days by the devil.

Six weeks of temptation. We read the story of the temptation, perhaps, in six minutes, but it lasted for nearly six weeks, *"for forty days."*

²And in those days He ate nothing, and afterward, when they had ended, He was hungry.

It does not appear, therefore, that Jesus was hungry while He was fasting. He was miraculously sustained during that period. After fasting, one looks for deeper spiritual feeling, and more holy joy. But the most prominent fact here is that *"afterward...He was hungry."* Think not that you have lost the benefit of your devout exercises when you do not at once feel it. Perhaps the very best thing that can happen to you, after much prayer, is a holy hunger. I do not mean a natural hunger, as it was with our Lord, but a blessed hungering after divine things. *"Blessed are those who hunger and thirst for righteousness, for they shall be filled"* (Matthew 5:6).

> *³And the devil said to Him, "If You are the Son of God, command this stone to become bread."*

Satan met the hungry Man, and suited the temptation to His present pangs, to His special weakness at that moment: *"If You are the Son of God, command this stone to become bread."* The devil suspected, and I think he knew, that Jesus was the Son of God, but he began his temptation with an *"if."* He hissed into the Savior's ear, *"If You are the Son of God."*

If you, believer, can be led to doubt your sonship, and to fear that you are not a son of God, Satan will have begun to win the battle. So he begins to storm the fort

179

royal of faith, *"If You are the Son of God."*
Our Lord is the Son of God, but He was
then suffering as our Substitute. In that
condition He was a lone and humble man.
What if I call Him "a common soldier in
the ranks"? Satan invites Him to work a
miracle of an improper kind on His own
behalf, but Jesus worked no miracle for
Himself.

Now, it may be, that the devil is trying
some of you tonight. You are very poor, or
business is going very awkwardly, and
Satan suggests that you should help yourself in an improper manner. He tells you
that you can get out of your trouble very
easily by some action which, although it
may not be strictly right, may not be so
very wrong after all. He said to Jesus, *"If
You are the Son of God, command this
stone to become bread."*

*⁴But Jesus answered him, saying, "It is
written,"*

That is Christ's sword. See how swiftly
He drew it out of its sheath. What a sharp
two-edged sword is this to be used against
Satan! You also, believer, have this powerful weapon in your hand. Let no man take

it from you. Believe in the inspiration of Scripture. Just now there is a fierce attack upon the Book of Deuteronomy. It is a very curious thing that all the texts Christ used during the temptation were taken out of Deuteronomy, as if that was to be the very armory out of which He would select this true Jerusalem blade, with which He should overcome the tempter. *"It is written. It is written."*

> [4]*"'Man shall not live by bread alone, but by every word of God.'"*

"God can sustain me without my turning the stone into bread. God can bring me through my trouble without my saying or doing anything wrong. I am not dependent upon the outward and visible." If you can feel like that, if you can appropriate the promise of God, and quote it to Satan saying, *"It is written,"* using it as Christ did, you will come off conqueror in the time of temptation even as He did.

> [5]*Then the devil,*

He tries Him again. Wave upon wave try to wash the Son of man off His feet.

⁵Taking him up on a high mountain, showed Him all the kingdoms of the world in a moment of time.

Skeptics have asked how that could be done. Well, they had better ask him who did it. He knows more about them, and they know more about him, than I do. He did it, I am sure, for here it is written that he *"showed Him all the kingdoms of the world in a moment of time."*

⁶And the devil said to Him, "All this authority I will give You, and their glory; for this has been delivered to me, and I give it to whomsoever I wish.

Does not he talk proudly in the presence of his Lord and Master? What an audacious dog he must have been to howl in the presence of Him who could have destroyed him by a look or a word if He had wished to do so!

⁷Therefore, if You will worship before me, all will be Yours.
⁸And Jesus answered and said to him, "Get behind me, Satan!"

The temptation annoyed Him, it was so foreign to His holy nature. It vexed His gracious spirit, so He cried out indignantly to the tempter: *"Get behind me, Satan."*

8"For it is written,"

Here flashed forth the sword again.

8"'You shall worship the Lord your God, and Him only you shall serve.'"

Then let us pay no reverence, no worship, to any but God. Consciences and minds are made for God alone. Before Him let us bow. But if all the world were offered to us for a moment's idolatry, let us not fall into the snare of the tempter.

9Then he brought Him to Jerusalem.

Satan now takes Christ to holy ground. Temptations are generally more severe there.

9Set him on the pinnacle of the temple,

The highest point of all; elevated high above the earth.

⁹And said to Him, "If You are the Son of God, throw yourself down from here.
¹⁰For it is written: 'He shall give His angels charge over you, to keep You,'
¹¹"And, 'In their hands they shall bear You up, lest You dash Your foot against a stone.'"

Now Satan tries to quote Scripture, as he can do when it suits his purpose, but he never quotes it correctly. You young brethren who go out preaching, mind that you do not imitate the devil by quoting part of a text or quoting Scripture incorrectly. He did it, however, with a purpose: not by misadventure or from forgetfulness, he left out the very necessary words, *"In all you ways." "He shall give his angels charge over you, to keep you in all your ways"* (Psalm 91:11). Satan left out those last four words, for it was not the way of a child of God to come down from a pinnacle of the temple headlong into the gulf beneath.

¹²And Jesus answered and said to him, "It has been said, 'You shall not tempt the Lord your God.'"

Do nothing presumptuously. Do nothing which would try to lead the Lord to act otherwise than according to His settled laws, which are always right and good.

> [13]Now when the devil had ended every temptation, he departed from Him until an opportune time.
> [14]Then Jesus returned in the power of the Spirit to Galilee.

He had not lost anything by the temptation, *"the power of the Spirit"* was still upon him.

> [14]And news of Him went out through all the surrounding region.
> [15]And he taught in their synagogues, being glorified by all.

He became popular. The people resorted to Him and were glad to hear Him. He who has had secret temptation and private conflict is prepared to bear open success without being elevated by it. Have you stood toe to toe with Satan? You will think little of the applause or of the attacks of your fellow men.